STALKED

To the hundreds of Australian women who tonight brace themselves for another terrifying episode at the hands of their own twisted stalker.

STALKED

EVERY WOMAN'S NIGHTMARE

CHRIS SMITH

First published in Australia in 2007 by
New Holland Publishers (Australia) Pty Ltd
Sydney • Auckland • London • Cape Town

www.newholland.com.au

14 Aquatic Drive Frenchs Forest NSW 2086 Australia
218 Lake Road Northcote Auckland New Zealand
86 Edgware Road London W2 2EA United Kingdom
80 McKenzie Street Cape Town 8001 South Africa

Copyright © 2007 in text: Chris Smith
Copyright © 2007 New Holland Publishers (Australia) Pty Ltd

All rights reserved. No part of this publication may be reproduced, stored in a retrieval system or transmitted, in any form or by any means, electronic, mechanical, photocopying, recording or otherwise, without the prior written permission of the publishers and copyright holders.

National Library of Australia Cataloguing-in-Publication Data:
Smith, Chris, 1962- .
Stalked: every women's nightmare

ISBN 9781741105278.

1. Stalking - New South Wales - Sydney - Case studies.
2. Stalkers - New South Wales - Sydney.
3. Criminal investigation - New South Wales - Sydney.
4. Women - Crimes against - New South Wales - Sydney. I. Title.

364.15099441

Publisher: Fiona Schultz
Production: Linda Bottari
Project Editor: Michael McGrath
Editor: Belinda Castles
Designer: Hayley Norman

CONTENTS

Introduction 6
Acknowledgments 8
Foreword by Jacqueline Milledge and Michael Kennedy 10

PART ONE: TERROR
Chapter 1: Praying for dawn 16
Chapter 2: Predator 30

PART TWO: TO TURN BACK TIME
Chapter 3: Himbos and him 42
Chapter 4: Entwined 53
Chapter 5: A psychotic mess 61
Chapter 6: Igniting evil 72
Chapter 7: Bashed 82

PART THREE: RELENTLESS
Chapter 8: In her face 92
Chapter 9: Not alone 98
Chapter 10: Interference 108
Chapter 11: A cry for sanity 118
Chapter 12: Prime time 127
Chapter 13: Last roll 140
Chapter 14: A litany of courage 151

PART FOUR: A LONG TIME COMING
Chapter 15: In the vice 162
Chapter 16: A mad mind 170
Chapter 17: Raising the gavel 178
Chapter 18: Remember me 188
Epilogue 190
About the author 192

INTRODUCTION

Having worked in an electronic storytelling medium for 26 years, it's not always the extreme manifestation of crime or behaviour that engrosses me enough to put the tale down in a book.

Sometimes it's the sheer commonality of the syndrome and its unimpeded damage that attracts me, that motivates me to delve further and tell as many people about it as possible.

According to the Australian Bureau of Statistics in 2005, almost 200,000 women were stalked in Australia. That's two or more stalking episodes from the same person. Forty per cent were stalked by a stranger and fourteen per cent by a previous partner.

This is the kind of anecdotal frequency I was fielding as an investigative journalist, but it was such a difficult crime to uncover and reveal. That was until I met Libby Masters, who in 1995 became the tragic victim of an incessant and obsessed stalker. Her predator's dysfunction was well on the way to wrecking one very promising life.

When Libby's case came to me, while I was working at *A Current Affair*, it was at the genesis of the television genre's hidden infra-red camera phase. It was only after this tale became televised, however, that I realised how essential it was to write this book. The stalker's tentacles were far-reaching. This was, without hyperbole, every woman's nightmare.

There is an intentional ten-year gap between the start and finish of this story ... after what the victims endured, they deserved such a respite. Therefore, today those same courageous women can either choose to revisit this horror in total anonymity or introduce those who now share their new lives to this tragic chapter in their past.

If, in some of the victims' recollections or my interpretation of them, some details have faded a little in that time lapse, I apologise in advance. I have done my very best to record what really happened between this serial stalker and his hapless victims.

I essentially want to highlight this frequently reported dysfunction to the widest possible readership. Stalking creates unreported and untold angst and horror for so many women across Australia. They deserve better protective legislation and sentencing, but, at a grassroots level, even greater attention from those that receive the panic call at the cop shop late at night. Never ignore the victim!

I hope that *Stalked* goes some way to highlighting the damaging fallout from such an insidious common obsession.

ACKNOWLEDGEMENTS

The long-suffering victims at the centre of this case deserve the ultimate thanks for their courage, firstly to fight back and secondly to be prepared to add very personal input into the telling of this story. Chief amongst them Libby Masters, who told me of her ordeal many more times than she was ever prepared to. She should be applauded for her uncanny ability to bounce back from repeated horror and still stick her neck out to seek closure and justice.

It was that mission—to shut her stalker from her life forever—which made her reticent to throw herself back into the telling of this story a decade after her anguish began. That to me will always be an entirely understandable reaction.

My appreciation goes too to the former detectives who joined in the hunt for the stalker. They later assisted the process with vital information and recently agreed to scan through an early manuscript.

To Matthew Condon—who not only connected me to Libby's plight, but continually encouraged me to write this book—I hope that we remain eternal mates.

To Managing Director Fiona Schultz, Publisher Martin Ford, Project Editor Michael McGrath, Editor Belinda Castles and Publicists Ian Dodd and Lotta Haegg, you've made disseminating this haunting story remarkably easy.

Thank you too to my old comrades at Channel Nine, who gave me opportunity and support, even when things didn't go to plan.

My thanks also to Warren Mallard, at Lyonswood Investigations, and Steve Packer, from the Barrington Group, who helped me tie up some important loose ends.

Acting NSW Chief Coroner Jacqui Milledge has had such a mammoth and high-profile caseload of late. Her insight into this menacing syndrome is gratefully accepted.

It's not such an impossible task researching and interviewing key players in a story, when you are totally consumed by the work. It is, however, an entirely different proposition a decade later, when the responsibility of marriage and toddlers compete with the writing of that story. This book would not have materialised without the patience and encouragement of my fabulously colourful wife Ally, who spent most of every second evening in 2006 without a husband. You are beautiful.

FOREWORD

Jacqueline Milledge

When I was a young probationary constable, in 1972, I lectured schoolchildren on the topic of 'stranger danger'. My warnings were sincere; my stories drawn from actual cases of child abuse and abduction. In those days, crimes against children, while abhorrent, were rarely exposed in the public arena. As I spoke to my young and captive audience, I was mindful that the likelihood of any of them becoming a victim at the hands of a stranger, although possible, was highly unlikely. Nonetheless, the message was important. They need only remember one simple rule; you can't trust people you don't know.

The children who listened intently to my stories will be adults themselves now, with children of their own. Sadly, too many of them, mostly women, will have learnt the hard way that there is a different kind of monster, someone who is no stranger to his victims. Someone the police lady failed to warn them about.

As a naïve police officer in the 1970s, I was never trained in the area of domestic violence. Generally police did not regard violence in the home as a serious problem. Police themselves reflected the attitudes of the wider community. I was taught that, at the slightest suggestion that you were going to apprehend the offending husband, the wife would turn and abuse you for interfering. Not all police adopted the attitude that it was simply a 'domestic' that could be resolved if the victim made some adjustment. Many of us could see it for the awful crime that it was.

Thankfully others in the community were lobbying to have this insidious and often deadly behaviour recognised and outlawed.

Australia's first women's refuge opened in 1972 in Glebe. Fully funded by the government, the Elsie Women's Refuge ensured there was a safe haven for women and children who were victims of domestic violence. The Sydney Rape Crisis Centre also opened its doors, supporting victims of sexual assault regardless of whether they reported their victimisation to police or chose to remain silent.

Silent victims no more! In the 1980s, police and the courts were encouraged and empowered by legislation to support the victim through the criminal justice process. Applications could be made to a court for an Apprehended Domestic Violence Order, prohibiting any behaviour that threatened, intimidated or harassed the victim. Anyone who breached the order could be arrested and brought before the courts to be dealt with according to law.

As a coroner I have, for many years, dealt with the brutal reality of what can go horribly wrong when relationships fail. From a single victim of homicide to entire families murdered by those who profess to love them so much they can't stand to live without them. Usually, at the end of their carnage, perpetrators turn the weapon on themselves to ensure they cannot be held to account in any mortal court.

In one such instance, during an inquest, I listened to a recording of a frantic telephone call a young woman made to '000'. She was pleading with police to come quickly to help her as her estranged boyfriend was breaking into her home with a high-powered rifle. As she begged the police for assistance, you could hear the sounds of breaking glass. He gained entry to the lounge room, where her stepfather placed himself between his daughter and her assailant. A shot rang out and her protector was wounded and left for dead. A second shot was closely followed by the screams of her dog that she had been holding in her arms. The little dog had been shot in the leg. The policeman asked, 'Are you alright?'

'No' she replied as she fell against the wall fatally wounded by the next bullet. The last shot heard on the tape was that of the perpetrator placing the rifle to his head.

Like Libby Masters, this victim had been stalked over time by her ex lover. Again, like Libby Masters, she did not receive an appropriate response from police when she reported her ongoing victimisation only days before the final encounter.

Given many women are stalked and intimidated by people they know, identifying the perpetrator is often easy. Marshalling sufficient evidence to support charging them is another story. It can be 'word against word' which accounts for the reluctance of some police to become involved. The concern is that, if it is not stopped, the level of violence can escalate resulting in the worst possible outcome for the victim, the police and at times the coroner.

Chris Smith has done a marvellous job in highlighting the brutal reality of stalking. These awful individuals who seek to control and torture their victims by constantly watching, following and intimidating their prey, are not simply 'pests' or 'jilted lovers'. They are highly motivated molesters who should be detected and dealt with.

Chris is to be commended for his vigilance and determination in ensuring Libby's perpetrator was exposed and prosecuted. It went far beyond investigative journalism. It is what I have come to expect from this award-winning journalist.

Jacqueline Milledge
Magistrate
Acting State Coroner

Dr Michael Kennedy

My good friend Chris Smith should be congratulated for exposing the dreadful social consequences associated with stalking. Stalkers choose to terrify and inflict the most debilitating punishment on their fellow human beings.

During almost 20 years as a detective in the NSW Police I dealt with numerous incidents of bullying and stalking—and witnessed the corrosive impact this horrible activity has on individuals, their families and the extended community. It's too easy to blame our legal system for this dreadful dilemma. From my standpoint, stalking is often a manifestation of an all-consuming patriarchy and aggressive competition, where every interaction must have a winner. Individuals become consumed with themselves, losing their community and collective responsibilities. Victims of stalking are often ignored by, or alienated from, their fellow human beings. Becoming involved in these matters requires a level of moral courage that is sadly missing in our aggressive and competitive society.

Some years ago, a well known Sydney criminal stalked a former girlfriend, threw bricks through her windows, slashed her tyres, intimidated witnesses and rang her at all hours of night and day. He poisoned her pets and sprayed her garden with weed killer. The victim and her new partner received almost no assistance from neighbours—who did not want to get involved. I believe the harassment only stopped when a number of men, who looked distinctly like police, made their presence felt around the culprit's car yard.

A besotted admirer stalked a colleague of mine. She came to the police station in a short skirt ... without knickers. She found his home phone number and address and tried to befriend his wife. My colleague was reduced to tears, asking for help before his marriage was ruined. I visited the woman who, fortunately, ceased the harassment. I believe the conversation between my colleague's wife and the female stalker also helped.

The new girlfriend of her ex partner, also female, stalked a young woman serving in the Army. She stole her car and tipped sugar into the petrol tank. She poured milk inside the vehicle in the heat of summer—the smell was unbelievable. The harassment only stopped after my female colleagues, who understood the dynamics of these relationships, visited the pair and clearly explained what would happen if the stalking did not cease. A quick description of the initiation ceremony awaiting female prisoners in our jails was an effective deterrent.

Stalking and bullying is not something peculiar to class, gender, religion or ethnicity. It is a plague upon our society with a corrosive impact on individuals that often manifests as other social and mental health issues.

The legal system is owned by its citizen's and only fails if we allow it to. The police should be the last resort in these matters—not the first. Most stalkers and bullies have little courage when they are confronted face to face. Unfortunately, most victims feel so powerless that they don't see this solution. Those who can and should help conveniently pretend to be oblivious to what's happening.

New rules and tougher penalties will not solve this issue for most victims. Stalkers and bullies obviously do not feel seriously threatened by sanctions. We must develop a multi-faceted, community-based initiative to deal with this problem. Perpetrators should not be able to insulate themselves through the inaction of their family, friends or associates.

Dr Michael Kennedy
School of Social Sciences
Bachelor of Policing
University of Western Sydney

PART ONE: TERROR

1

PRAYING FOR DAWN

It was dusk on a Sunday night and, as Libby Masters opened the front door of her tiny cottage in Mosman, she could smell the stale January air escaping from her hallway. She closed the door behind her and was jolted by a sobering thought. She stared at the deadlock on the back of the door. She'd completely forgotten to change the locks—and she knew that Phillip Hopkins had retained the spare set of keys he'd cut for himself a week ago. All feelings of safety and resolution evaporated. She stood for what seemed like minutes, staring at that lock, knowing she was powerless to turn back time and correct her mistake.

She turned from the door in slow motion, entering the bedroom without taking a breath. Her bag was filled with clothes she'd worn during her break down south. She wished she was still there, on Anthony's veranda or sipping a coffee in Zucchero's cafe bar. But the flashback to Melbourne, December 1995, to a place of comfort and security, was enough to jolt her out of her fear. Libby wasn't running any longer. Her fright gave way to determination. It was all she had. She marched into every room in the house, talking out loud, ensuring she was alone and at peace. 'No more!' she said loudly, comforted by her own voice.

There was much to be done before bedtime and it would be done, no matter how vulnerable his ghostly presence in the house made her feel. Most of the small pokey rooms, crammed with quaint, familiar furniture, needed tidying and cleaning. It was only when she came across remnants of her last violent episode with Hopkins that her momentum faltered for a moment. There were still fragments of glass and porcelain in the fibres of her lounge room rug, the result of one of his most recent outbursts.

She continued with her task. The broom and dustpan got a good workout, as banging and scraping echoed through her home, ricocheting off the timber floor and high, ornate ceilings. The can of Mr Sheen was as good as empty after she set upon the table and bench tops. The bathroom and kitchen didn't escape the treatment either. The vacuum cleaner was full to capacity after 30 minutes gliding around every room in the house. As much as performing a spring clean, Libby was eradicating the emotional mess that had dominated her life for so long. As she cleaned, she talked to reassure herself.

After picking at a plate of cheese from the refrigerator, Libby rested on the lounge and turned on the television to catch the Sunday night movie. One channel was screening a horror movie and she couldn't help but smile. She switched to find something more palatable and came across a familiar flick—just what she needed.

An hour passed and during a commercial break, Libby went into her bedroom and turned on the lamp. Those creaking floorboards seemed loud tonight and she vowed to prune that frangipani, which scraped repeatedly against the window of her bedroom. She opened the drawer of her side table, found her nightie and laid it across her bed. Closing the blinds at the front window, she noticed the dimly lit trees in her front yard swaying with the breeze. The frangipani's branches knocked gently against the frame.

The mere thought of a cool change raised the hairs on the back of her neck and goose bumps prickled on her arms and legs. She removed her shirt and shorts and undid her bra—it was rubbing against her shoulders after her whirlwind cleaning frenzy. She tossed the clothes into the basket behind her door. She picked up the nightie and slipped it over her head, lifting her arms as the silk slid over her shoulders and down to her thighs. She switched off the light and went back out to the kitchen for a glass of water. The shuddering of water through the straining copper pipes startled her. Her right knee smacked against the sink cupboard.

As the water rushed into the glass, a flicker of yellow light reflected briefly on the right side of the tap. She turned towards the window quickly. She tried to focus her vision, peering into the pitch black of her small, leafy rear yard. Frowning, she stood still, unable to work out where the flicker had come from. She watched, totally still for twenty seconds, not breathing, until she saw another flicker of light flash between the bushes on the back fence. The silhouettes of trees and branches tossed in the darkness. The breeze had become a wind and the flicker appeared again and then again. Her glass slipped in her hand, clanging against the sink, scaring her witless.

She crossed her arms, wrapping them around her shoulders and across her breasts. She was cold, close to shaking and her heart pumped hard. She lunged at the kitchen window, releasing the curtain ties to cover the view. It was pointless—the curtains were thin white lace, transparent. Libby shuffled quickly into the lounge and dropped the wooden venetians, tightening the slats. But the slats left gaps. If he was out there, he could see her every move.

She rechecked the deadlock on the back door, then switched off the light and the television, standing silently in the middle of the ever-narrowing room. Her body was shaking. What should she do? She listened to the wind between the trees and waited for the next sign to confirm what she feared—that Hopkins was armed with the dark again and was slowly moving along her back fence.

Fifteen minutes passed. Then a muffled thud struck her bathroom window, the only window without any covering. What the hell was that? Could he be trying to break the window to get inside?

'Oh God, stop it, Phillip. Stop it please,' she pleaded softly. Through the venetians she saw vividly the shadow of a man passing by the window. Her breath left her body. She backed down the corridor, not knowing where to hide. Another thud hit the kitchen window; it rattled violently. The fright made her jump 30 centimetres off the ground. 'Oh my God! Please go away. Stop it!' she yelled.

Replying to her scream, a thud rattled the spare room window and a flash of light beamed into the corridor less than a metre away.

'That's it,' she said as she ran back into the darkened lounge room to pick up the telephone. After knocking her leg against the telephone table, she grappled with the receiver before dialling triple-0. The reply took what seemed like an eternity, but in reality the operator came on the line in less than ten seconds.

'Please, I need the police,' Libby begged.

'What's wrong, Madam? Where are you?' asked the calm female voice on the other end.

'He's in my yard. He's mad. He'll hurt me again and he can get inside! Please, can you please get the police here quickly?'

'Who's there, Madam?'

'My boyfriend. No, my ex-boyfriend, Phillip Hopkins,' she said.

'How do you know he's there, Madam?'

'Oh please believe me, it's him,' she said in a louder voice, her eyes now welling with tears of frustration.

Realising Hopkins might be listening, she lowered her voice to tell the operator her address and demanded that a police car be sent around. She dropped to the floor and huddled against the lounge, rocking back and forth on the rug, anxiously awaiting his next move. Tears rolled freely down her face as she jammed her chin firmly between her knees. She was as cold as ice but wasn't prepared to move to find a jumper or a dressing gown to keep warm. Again, the light appeared through the bathroom window and remained for several seconds before going out.

'You are a psychopath, Phillip!' she yelled as loud as she could. 'This breaches your AVO again, you idiot. They'll send you to jail for this, you bastard!'

Seconds later there was a knock at the front door. She gripped her knees tighter. She was not going to open the door to a violent and enraged Hopkins. 'As if I don't know who's there, you weak bastard.'

Two replies came at once. Laughter broke out from the rear yard as a male voice from the other side of the door told her that it was the police. They were at opposite ends of the property, but he was still here—they could catch him if they were quick. She ran down the corridor, grabbed her keys en route and opened the front door. Two officers with stony faces stood before her. 'What seems to be the problem, madam?' one of the officers asked.

'He's still here, in the backyard. Please come through, quick.'

The pair hesitated, then looked at each other, before following her through the house, waiting while she found the keys to the back door. She floundered, unable to find the right key.

'Sorry, it's here somewhere,' she smiled as she looked back at the pair. Her smile disappeared. She felt sick and alone again.

'That's okay. You're Libby, are you?' asked the other officer, detecting her awkwardness.

'Yes, Libby Masters, and the guy out there is Phillip Hopkins,' she replied.

She found the key and opened the door, stepping back to allow the officers to enter the backyard first. The officers marched out, switching on the back light as they passed. Libby stood at the doorway as the men walked the perimeters of the yard, pointing their black steel torches over the fence.

'I think he came in from where you are there,' she said, nodding towards their position at the back fence, 'That's where I saw his light.'

'Nothing here now,' one of them replied.

'He was here when you came to the front door though, he was laughing. He's breaching the AVO I have out on him, you know. It's a direct breach being here.'

The officers returned, speaking quietly as they grew closer. One handed her a brightly coloured plastic basketball—a child's toy. They had found it by one of the fences. Libby took it in one hand and tried to think where she'd seen it before.

'That must have been what he threw at the windows,' Libby said, 'I can give you his address if you want. You can track down the case.'

'What good is that?' said the more abrupt officer. 'You told the emergency operator you couldn't verify that it was this Hopley character.'

'Hopkins his name is and yes, I know that. But you don't know him, it had to be him.'

'Well, that's not going to get us a warrant,' the officer said, slapping his torch in the palm of his hand. 'We need more than that. A ball doesn't prove he's breached his AVO. I can't see any reason for us to hang around here any longer; he's obviously been scared off and won't come back tonight—if it was him. We'll camp up the end of the street for a short while and see what happens.'

Libby was dumbstruck, embarrassed and totally helpless. This could happen again and again and there was nothing she could do. The two police officers made their way down the corridor and out the front door.

'If you want to make a statement, get down to the North Sydney Police Station sometime tomorrow, I'm on at three,' said the second officer, the friendlier of the two, who handed Libby a card. 'My name's Haddock. You can have a go at arguing the case for breach of AVO if you like.'

'An AVO should be enforceable shouldn't it? Especially as it's based on an assault? He nearly killed me,' Libby said. 'He keeps breaching it and getting away with it!'

'AVOs are a waste of time, that's what they are,' the first officer interjected.

'Hey!' scolded Haddock, then more softly, 'It's an Apprehended Domestic Violence Order Libby, that's all. You can't tell a court it's been breached without proof, but if you come across something, or have him confess to it, or others claim he was here, you could get him put away for a little while.'

'I've been through this over and over again. I've made so many statements. I'm sick of wasting my time.'

'Listen, come down to the station tomorrow and I'll explain everything. Coming to your home like this may force a magistrate to get tougher with him. Courts are a bit of a lottery but I may be able to help.'

'Okay, I might do that.'

They left. Libby locked her door and turned out all the lights. She wanted to see but remain unseen. She stretched the telephone cord into her bedroom and positioned the phone precariously on her side table. She barricaded herself into the bedroom with an old Federation lock and key.

She felt a little safer, a little warmer, but was in no mood for sleep. Pulling out a novel from the top bedside drawer, she climbed under the doona.

The wind was now howling outside and all she could hear was her heart pounding and the frangipani scraping her bedroom window. She tried to read entirely under the doona using a book-light, but her mind was constantly wandering, reliving the past terrifying hour and planning her next move in case he dared to return.

She tried to read some more, but found herself nodding off and then jolting awake each time her book closed. She heard all the noises outside: the scratches on the window, the rattling of a tin roof a few doors up and the odd car, driving past her house. She could have sworn several engines sounded just like Phillip's Laser and slowed down directly outside her front fence before speeding away.

It was now three o'clock in the morning and Libby knew that she'd only be able to catch three hours sleep at most. She wished it was earlier so she could sleep longer, in order to cope with her return to work. However, she was still so frightened that she was praying for dawn at the same time. She longed for the birds to begin chirping outside, signalling the start of a new, bright day, without the darkness and terror of the night. She placed her book on the table next to the bed, but baulked at turning off the reading light and decided to leave it on to keep her company. She cuddled up under the doona and was determined to fall asleep.

Her half-sleep was invaded by a loud crash, followed by a second crash. She tensed up and remained hidden under the covers.

No, not again, please, she thought to herself.

Then she heard a firm knock at the back door. She was beginning to sweat under the doona, her body shaking. A knock struck the bathroom window, followed by another knock at the kitchen window. Silence for ten seconds, then a knock at the spare room window, then a knock at the front window next to her bed. He was running around the damn house. She closed her eyes tight. She was trapped. He could enter whenever he wanted.

A loud thump came from the front door, then a knock at the bedroom window seconds later. She knew he'd have his torch on, that she'd see silhouettes at every window, but she didn't dare raise her head above the covers. They remained so tightly shut she could see stars in the black abyss.

'You're going to pay, Libby. You can't throw us away,' came the whispered snarl from outside her front window. There was no doubt now, if she'd ever had any, that this was Phillip. She refused to reply, for fear of encouraging him or provoking him to enter her house in a rage. She had no defence, no plan, no way of stopping the knocking. What good would ringing the police do? Would they really come back after the first time?

Hopkins was circling the house, tapping and knocking on all the doors, all the windows. It lasted for twenty minutes, interspersed with one word, 'Libby', over and over and over again. He allowed just enough time between assaults on the house to startle Libby with each new sound. She felt as though she was in a horror movie, suffering an unremitting campaign of intimidation.

He doesn't actually want to come in, she thought. He's stalking me.

The word exploded into her consciousness. This was stalking. It was not merely a case of making her scared; she was being stalked, like she'd seen in those tele-movies and, once or twice, on the television news. She'd read how it had led to assaults and even murder. She remembered the row in the newspapers recently about laws designed to stop stalking, to prevent these personal campaigns of terror developing into violence. She was now more frightened than ever—and overheating, wet with fear. All of a sudden, the noises ceased.

Libby woke without sensing even a whisper of breeze. A bird chirped in a nearby tree. The creep must have gone; it must be dawn. More birds joined in the chorus. Three cars drove by. She slowly pulled her head out from under the doona. By now she was lathered in sweat. Slowly she unclenched her eyelids; they'd been shut so tightly for so long, that she had to peel them apart. Light crept through the slats in her venetians. Dawn had arrived like a rescue worker in a storm.

She lay motionless as the birds came out to play, as more cars drove by, as the sound of babies' cries pierced the air. As the minutes ticked by, day broke and her fear was extinguished.

What the hell do I do now? she thought. Who can help me? How do I stop him? Where do I go? Her colleague and friend Shane Bailey, who'd stood up to Phillip on her behalf before, was interstate on assignment. Who will truly believe me? Why am I here, in this shitful position?

Libby began sobbing; her eyes were already sore and red from lack of sleep. She felt imprisoned—alone and terrorised. Her sobbing lasted almost 30 minutes, the long culmination of a full week of restrained tension and anxiousness. It was usually the most wonderful part of the day for her, the sun lifting her out of bed and bracing her for the day ahead, but she didn't care anymore; she just didn't care.

Her morning at the office, where she worked as an executive assistant, a job she usually loved, began disastrously: a cranky boss, wisecracking colleagues, a coffee spill and paranoia every time the phone rang. Libby knew she had nowhere to hide. He would undoubtedly track her movements from work if she left again for Melbourne and Anthony's apartment. There was no way she wanted Anthony embroiled in this mess, the nights of stalking and the threats to anyone within cooee of her. And Anthony's busy schedule meant that she'd be even more alone there than she would be here.

Eventually her mother decided, unusually, to ring her at work. Libby made it through 30 seconds of the conversation before breaking down. They decided that Libby would take the rest of the day off, pack up some things and move in with her parents at Balgowlah that afternoon.

The Masters' home, like Libby's, was more a typical Sydney cottage than a house. The block was narrow but quite long, with a fence out front. Most of the structure was weatherboard, apart from the front rooms, which were obviously part of the original building; a standard, brick Californian bungalow. The cottage was single storey and freestanding, with a newly renovated rear section including a large television room which led onto a laundry, spare room and veranda. As soon as Libby walked into the television room behind her mother, she saw immediately that the large glass doors onto the veranda had no curtains or coverings. All she could think of was how exposed she would be in the dark of night.

The backyard had a shed deep in the corner and a barbecue to one side. The back fence bordered another backyard and the area was covered in tall trees and shrubs. It was relatively dense terrain for a suburb so close to the city.

'You can have the spare room love,' her mother said as she opened the door and walked to the window to let in some air. 'We've put your old bed in here, but I didn't think it'd be used so soon.'

'Thanks, Mum.'

Libby's face was pale, her eyes puffy. She was wrecked, in every way. She threw down her two overnight bags and climbed onto the bed. Her mother told her when her father was due home. The last thing she heard before nodding off to sleep was something about when dinner would be served.

When Libby awoke, it was pitch-dark. The blackness startled her and she scrambled to turn on the bedside lamp. There was a window on one side of the room, cloaked by a thick curtain. On the other side, there was a row of four small push-out, slat windows high up towards the ceiling. She peered through bleary eyes at an old digital clock beside the bed. It was eleven—she calculated that she'd just slept for nine hours.

Being in the same house as her parents made her long to go back in time, back to that familiar school-age safety zone—back to a time when she still had a chance to avoid the mistakes of adulthood, namely any association with Phillip Hopkins.

'Sorry I slept so long,' Libby said as she stumbled into the dining room, where her father was reading and her mother was mending a pair of his work shorts.

'That's okay love,' her mother said.

'You'll sleep your life away girl,' said her father in a cynical but playful tone, his head only partially turning towards his daughter.

Libby's father stood to give her a kiss with a smile. Alex Masters never interfered when it came to his daughter's many boyfriends, but he'd never been keen on the 'rich kid', Phillip Hopkins, and he had mentioned it. He didn't bring up her problems, though, that night at their late dinner, while Libby picked at what was left of her shrunken and dry plate of roast lamb and vegetables.

Libby spent two quiet nights at her parent's home at Balgowlah, before venturing out for dinner with her girlfriend Sarah on the Wednesday. They didn't dine at their favourite Thai restaurant in nearby Neutral Bay; Libby was too fragile to be anywhere remotely accessible to Hopkins.

They travelled that night across Sydney Harbour, to a seafood restaurant at Brighton-le-Sands—out of the way and well clear of trouble. Libby's mind wandered all evening. The events of Sunday night still shook her deeply, her feelings resurfacing as she told the story to her best friend. She was back in the Mosman house, back under the tyranny of Hopkins.

As their dinner wound up and the waiter delivered the bill to their table, Libby's attention was distracted by a flash of light from the side window of the establishment, the side that faced Botany Bay, onto the dark expanse of water off the beach. It must be a boat on the way to a mooring, she thought. Seconds later his face appeared, there at the window, smiling broadly, directly at Libby. His expression seemed pleased by Libby's shock, but at the same time angry. Sarah followed Libby's gaze, catching only a glimpse of a man walking past the window, but she could see from Libby's face who he was.

A glass of mineral water slipped from Libby's frozen hand, crashing onto the table. She ran immediately to the bathroom. How could she leave now? He would follow her again, hunting her way beyond her usual geographical boundaries.

Eventually she returned to the table. Now Sarah was living Libby's hell and could more than merely sympathise with what she was going through. After paying the bill, they left, moving cautiously towards Sarah's vehicle. It wasn't parked too far away, but each step was taken with trepidation. They drove away without saying a word and kept looking around, in all the rear mirrors, to see if Hopkins was tailing them. As they made their way through the city and eventually over the Harbour Bridge, Libby sighted his car, three behind theirs. He hadn't given up. But as they emerged onto Falcon Street, a Random Breath Test unit pulled him over and ended the chase. The women were greatly relieved.

'Anything I do now, Sarah, is only going to piss him off more and add to his anger. He'll just hound me until I crack,' said Libby in a resigned tone.

Sarah didn't reply. She didn't have the conviction to argue otherwise. Her sighting of Hopkins wasn't concrete enough to help Libby prove that he'd breached his bail conditions again. Sarah was pragmatic about Libby's options. 'You have to get help, real help—an investigator, or have the police put surveillance on him, or find something else that he's done.'

'If I don't do something, I'm afraid he'll hurt me again. If I do take more serious action, it may make it all worse. I don't know what to do … ' Libby turned towards the car window to conceal her emotion.

He didn't return that night, but still Libby spent those hours sick with fear. There was no way he could have followed her; there was no sign of him, but if he was prepared to tail her best friend, he was capable of anything.

The following night, she arrived at Balgowlah around ten o'clock, tired and ready for bed. It was an abnormally warm night and she felt clammy and in need of a cool shower. The spare room had its own tiny ensuite, the extension designed by the previous owners as a kind of granny flat for visitors. The window was frosted but had no curtains nor blinds. She was aching to wash and put her head on the pillow. She stood under the shower without even bothering to soap herself. Resting her head against the wall tiles, she let the water pound her shoulders and back. Her eyes were shut tight, her arms hung down by her sides like lead weights and she was in mental limbo, vacant in a cloud of exhaustion.

Suddenly she heard what she thought sounded like a strange thud in the small passage outside her window between the house and the adjoining fence—like a large cat jumping from a ledge. She turned 180 degrees towards the window. It was impossible to see anything; the light inside blinded her. She froze, wondering whether the noise was her newly acquired paranoia or truly something to be worried about. If it was more than a cat out there, the outline of her naked body was on show for anyone to see. Instinctively, Libby wrapped her arms around her breasts. Her heart pounded as it had done on Sunday night. She did not dare move, waiting for another sound—a cat or a possum.

My parents are in the same house, for God's sake, she thought.

She quickly turned off the taps. The only sound now was the tapping of water droplets falling from her wet body onto the tiles below. Her parents were in bed and she wasn't prepared to wake them for what might only be a neighbour's tomcat on the prowl.

She stepped out of the shower, taking small breaths, so as to keep her focus on any further noises outside. She wiped the water off her chest, stomach, thighs, legs and then her back, placing the towel slowly over the steel hook behind the door. She walked out into the darkened bedroom naked and peered up to the small windows to her left.

'Oh God!' she yelled.

High up, like an animal in the fork of a tree, directly outside the windows, she spotted two shiny eyes staring down at her through the terrifying mask of what looked like a black balaclava. The eyes were so shiny, so watery ... they looked straight through her like a laser beam.

She threw herself to the ground, hiding behind the bed. Another thud followed, then a series of footsteps in the grass several metres away. They tailed off until she couldn't hear them anymore. She stayed down, in a foetal position tucked close to the base of the bed.

The door of her bedroom flew open and she yelped in terror again, crawling backwards against the bedside drawers, knocking the digital clock and lamp to the ground in one action.

It was her father, hair ruffled, wearing only his underwear and a worn dressing gown.

'What's wrong?' He'd clearly run from his bedroom to this end of the house.

'He was here. That bastard was perving at me—he knows where I am,' Libby said, bursting into tears.

'Are you sure?'

'Yes!'

Alex left the room, opened the glass doors to the veranda, switched on the backyard lights and jogged to the rear fence some twenty metres away. In the meantime Libby had pulled on her dressing gown and walked out into the television room, standing at the door to wait for her father. After several minutes he walked back onto the veranda, his eyes focused on his feet. And then he walked right past Libby and through to the television room. 'Did the sensor light go on?' he asked angrily.

'I don't think so, no. But I'm not sure.'

'Well, how could he be there then?' he said loudly before walking off down the corridor.

'Dad! He was here; you don't believe me, do you?' Libby called after him.

'Not really, no,' came his reply. 'Think about it Libby: no sensor light, no bloody boyfriend in the backyard. You're stressed. I know that.'

Libby slammed the glass doors closed, locking the clasp tight and leaving the outside light on. She stormed back into her bedroom, slamming the door. She fell onto her bed and began sobbing, her face firmly buried in the pillow. She cried herself to sleep.

2

PREDATOR

It was eight o'clock in the morning and Libby was standing at the counter of the North Sydney Police Station, in pursuit of Senior Constable Haddock. After talking to her friend Shane, who, like Sarah, had also witnessed Hopkins' behaviour first-hand, Libby had decided to use the tools she had at her disposal; she would take up the offer of investigating the possibility of finding a magistrate who would be tough on Hopkins' constant breach of his Apprehended Violence Order.

He'd become unstoppable. Libby's work was suffering, the hours after work were a nightmare and the more she ran away, the more ardently he chased her down. Officer Haddock drew up the paperwork, gathering the material, such as it was, into a statement, and organised the court date. It was routine stuff for Haddock, but a serious step for Libby, a stranger to the world of law and order.

'What if he ignores this again?' Libby asked politely from her seat in the interview room.

'Well, with Shane Bailey's word, you've been able to prove he's turned up within 100 metres of you. There's ambiguity over whether he just happened to be in the same area coincidentally, but his arrival at your home, that's a breach and a half; it's a more significant breach of orders and privacy to some magistrates,' said Haddock. 'Don't worry Libby, once the order is out, they'll bail him up and it'll scare the daylights out of him. This is serious. These are orders of the court.'

Libby remained unconvinced.

Her appearance at North Sydney Court was held a few days later and Libby found herself in a sausage factory system. She met the prosecutor for no more than a few minutes; the case itself was a matter of handing up a small file of forms to the magistrate, who barely peered over his spectacles to witness the victim in the proceedings.

'AVO breached at her home—get him in here,' mumbled the magistrate, after glancing quickly over one of the pages. 'Sheriff!'

The case was over before Libby even had a chance to sit down and take in the Victorian decor of the courtroom. 'That's it,' Haddock whispered, taking her by the arm.

'That's it?' Libby asked, baffled. 'He didn't give a damn!'

According to Rowan Haddock, there would be a warrant for Hopkins' arrest. He'd be brought to the nearest police station and made to appear before the magistrate. Libby was also encouraged to call the police as soon as she saw him again. They had his home address at Cremorne and knew where he worked, so his apprehension was just a matter of time.

Libby's entry into the Australian justice system seemed simultaneously bland and bizarre. In spite of the warrant for his arrest, she couldn't help but think that she was the only one taking Hopkins' stalking seriously—that she was the only one watching her back. That realisation steeled her for what might lie ahead …

Libby could only imagine Phillip's surprise when the police came knocking at his door.

Libby's mother insisted she remain at Balgowlah at least until the weekend. She had endured so much. The police interview and court case were reigniting the embers of Libby's fear and Jan Masters was concerned for her daughter's health. She needed to rest before she returned to Mosman. For her part, Libby wasn't looking forward to returning home. The memories were still fresh in her mind, her house a reminder of his knocking, yelling and stalking. It wasn't so long ago that she'd been cruelly coaxed into having sex with him … It was Libby's turning point.

On Friday, Libby's last day before moving back into her Mosman semi, she'd turned down an invitation to join the girls at the Oaks Hotel. Partying–especially having to contend with strange men—was the last thing on her to–do list. Her parents had gone out to see friends—a regular outing that her mother would have cancelled if not for Libby's insistence that they not fuss over her.

Libby was prepared to go one extra yard in her efforts to defend herself. She went to the kitchen and grabbed her mother's largest kitchen knife from the block, then took it into her room and laid it down next to the bedside lamp. It shone under the ceiling light, as threateningly as she intended.

At around ten she turned off the lounge room light, checked all the windows and doors and went to her room. She felt a little apprehensive, as she did as a child when her mother and father retired for the night. She was never fond of complete darkness and her childhood fear returned now.

Libby decided to take a shower—she was determined to carry on as usual and not to allow Hopkins to dictate her life by remote control. She glanced up at the row of slat-windows near the ceiling. The oak tree outside was swaying in the evening breeze. There was the odd rattle and scraping noise coming from the bushes outside but nothing to worry herself about.

She began removing her clothes. It was no longer an ordinary, thoughtless process. She was a wary woman now, protective of her space and, in particular, her body. She pulled her T-shirt up over her shoulders and dropped it on the floor beside her. She undid the fly on her shorts and slid them down over her hips and past her knees. She grabbed at the rear of her bra and undid the clasp, quickly pulling the straps down over her arms, and tossed it onto the bed. She removed her underpants just as quickly. How could something so automatic, so natural, be so deliberate now—so nerve wracking?

Libby began the process of thinking her way through her fear. She knew she had good reason to be proud of the courage she had shown by prosecuting the AVO order. What it meant in reality was yet to be determined. Libby found an FM music station on the old portable stereo player above her chest of drawers and some familiar classics put her instantly into a more relaxed state. She jumped confidently into the shower and soaped herself until her body was covered in a thick lather. The warm water was a welcome tonic and she felt more relaxed than at any time in recent memory. After washing herself and turning the taps off, Libby stepped from the shower and dried her body all over. She felt better. There was a sense of calm in the room, solitude without fear.

Back in her room, towel in hand, she stood in front of the mirror and squeezed her hair dry.

Libby watched herself standing in the soft light of the moon. She looked down at her body and was determined she'd never allow another man to see her this way so easily again. She had a naturally beautiful figure but hadn't had the time or inclination of late to remind herself of the fact, to dwell on anything that might help boost her self-esteem.

She slowly dropped the towel to her feet and lay on the bed. She was a little drowsy from her busy day and she started thinking of the last time she had lain like this, naked and relaxed, back at Mosman. It had been a long while since she'd stopped and unwound. It had been with Phillip—a very different Phillip, the one who had made her feel so very good. He'd seemed so caring, so complimentary of who she was and how she appeared. She closed her eyes and drifted.

In her semi-consciousness, she could picture them together. His strong upper body engulfed her slender frame. His large hands held her shoulders. Her breath and heartbeat intensified. She could smell him, his aftershave, imagine his lips, his hair. She felt no love or attachment, only lust. For a moment, the memories of their time together were not so harrowing. She could recall his breathing almost precisely. His smell was palpable. It felt real. It was as if he was there.

Her eyes flew open and Hopkins was indeed there, two metres away, outside the large window to the backyard, smiling broadly through that horrifying black balaclava. She'd forgotten to draw the curtain on that window when she first walked in; it had been too dark to notice. She screamed and struggled to get up off the bed. He banged on the widow and yelled. 'You were thinking about me weren't you? How good is that? You were, weren't you? Don't fight it.'

'Get away! Go away!' Libby screamed as she ran into the bathroom to find another towel. 'You're sick! This is against the law, you bastard.'

She was desperate to close the curtains, but in that terrifying split second, she couldn't bring herself to correct her mistake. It would have meant flinging herself closer to him, although a pane of glass stood between them. She reached for the towel and wrapped it around her shaking body, retreating to the bathroom. Hopkins remained at the window, bashing the pane and yelling profanities, interspersed by declarations of love. She slid to the floor, pressing her hands against her ears. Still he bashed, then knocked, in a constant, infuriating fashion. At times the bashing was so hard it sounded as if it would shatter the window in its frame. After perhaps twenty seconds, she regained her composure and ran from the room, past his glaring eyes and into the lounge room where she reached for the telephone. Dialling triple-0, she turned her face away from the glass doors, to where he'd repositioned himself to watch her.

'Please come! Please come!' she yelled at the operator.

That familiar frustration followed, as the detached voice at the other end of the line coolly asked for details.

'Who's coming, Libby? I'm here—you don't need anyone else!' Phillip yelled. 'You're mine and always will be. You know that. You know that, you bloody bitch. I will hound you until you realise what you've lost. And you will.'

'The police are on their way, Libby,' the operator said. 'Just remain calm.'

She ran to the front of the house, standing in the corridor away from exterior windows. Suddenly she remembered the knife—she swore at herself for having forgotten it earlier. It was too late now. She shook in the cold like a freezing animal.

Then, the yelling, the banging, the abuse ended. The house was deathly silent. She looked around the corner and Hopkins' silhouette was no longer on the patio. But where was he? He didn't leave in peace when he stalked her at Mosman and there was no reason to think he would now. She could feel him close, glanced from window to window in search of his face.

Libby eventually shuffled through the lounge room into the bedroom, where she grabbed her T-shirt and jeans swiftly before running back to her hiding place at the front of the house. He might have been peering through one of her windows, but she couldn't bring herself to check. Libby stepped into her jeans and pulled her T-shirt on. She had nowhere to move, nowhere to go.

Small, far-off footsteps were heard at the front of the house and they grew louder as they approached the front door. Surely this was the police. She was standing only a metre away from the door and was tempted to walk away. But it had to be the police, the footsteps were too clear; there'd been no attempt to hide them. So she waited, her teeth chattering. But there was no knock at the door. She heard a key being inserted into the keyhole and watched in horror as the door handle twisted clockwise.

A male voice came through the door: 'Libby, why are the police here?'

She sighed with relief. It was her father with two burly officers trailing after him into the hallway.

'Ma'am,' said the first, his cap under his arm.

Libby managed a small smile and nodded.

'Well, what's going on? Not the mystery man again?' her father said.

'He's not a mystery man, Dad.' Libby spoke to the first policeman, 'I think he may still be here, officer, out the back. Come and I'll show you.'

The two policemen scoured the backyard, over the fences, behind the shed, up along the side of the house and back over the neighbouring fences again. Libby's mother stood by her daughter on the patio and held her tight. It was useless; Hopkins had either vanished or he'd found a well-disguised hiding place. Libby needed to prove he'd been stalking, if there was even a way of doing such a thing. It seemed hopeless—this was his modus operandi; he'd frighten the living daylights out of her, get away with it, then do it again, just for the thrill of it.

'I'm sorry she dragged you gentlemen all the way out here to play hide and seek,' her father joked. 'But she's had an ugly break-up recently and, well, all is not well I fear.'

Libby had no comeback. The officers offered a half smile in reply and then bid their farewells.

'Before you go,' Libby said, 'I want it noted that I truly believe he was here, because he was.'

'Okay, ma'am, not a problem. It's noted,' said one of the officers, pulling out his notebook and pen.

After the officers had left, Libby refused to go anywhere near her bedroom. Her mother agreed to stay up with her, until the sun came up if need be. Libby regarded the dawn as the only sign that the coast was clear. She was prepared to watch as many corny repeated American soapies as she needed to, until she was satisfied Hopkins would not return. Each time her mother nodded off, Libby cleared her throat to keep her awake. They raided the tea tin until it was empty and kept the lights on throughout the house.

As soon as the birds began chirping and the darkness outside was softened by the beginning of day, she said thanks to her mum, kissed her on the forehead and went back to her bedroom to sleep. Sleeping in daylight shifts was the only combat tactic that she could conjure up for now.

After sleeping until two in the afternoon, she called Shane and asked him to come to Balgowlah. He'd just returned from interstate and was eager to catch up with Libby. When he arrived, she gave him a run-down of recent events.

'What do I do, Shane? What the hell do I do? I can't live anywhere without Phillip finding me. He scares me senseless. The police are no help; my father and now maybe mum think I'm overreacting and all I can do to stop this stalker is stay up all night and sleep all day. I'll lose my job soon and one night, somewhere, he'll get me again and I know he'll hurt me. He's already done it. He's hopelessly obsessed. How can I be this helpless?'

The pair was sitting on the patio watching the harsh afternoon sun sink in the west over the back fence. Both sat forward nervously in their seats. Libby leaned her head on her hand, partially covering her face.

'Well, I don't think I have any magical solutions—but you could stay at my place,' he said.

It was the second time Shane had made the offer. Libby instantly detected awkwardness between them. Was he being helpful, or just using her problems as a way of starting up some kind of relationship? Or was she so paranoid that she couldn't even trust her closest friends? She gave it little further thought and concluded that she was being unfair to Shane.

'I could, I guess,' she said finally. 'But that's just putting a bandaid on the situation,' she said.

'Why? Do you think he'll keep doing this?' asked Shane. 'Unless he's a dead set professional at this stuff. He's a sick mongrel—incredibly jealous and angry all rolled up into one ... but he's too good at it as well.'

'A professional?'

'Yeah. He seems it—never gets caught for one. I wouldn't be surprised if he's perfected the art of stalking by doing it over and over again to other women.' Shane said, 'Maybe he's doing this to multiple women at the same time and has done it many times before.'

'A serial stalker? He does get a thrill out of it. The more frightening the episodes for me, the bigger the thrill. He's so sick. It could also explain where he gets to sometimes, when he just doesn't turn up. It would explain a lot of things, a lot of why he just went missing in action so often when we were together. Nights of nothing—and no proper explanation.'

'The way you describe his movements,' Shane continued, 'the way he finds where you're staying, the way he remains undetected, knows exactly how to avoid the sensor lights, creeps up on you without you knowing ... well, maybe he's an old hand at this—a self-trained stalker.'

Libby looked at Shane, stunned.

'You're exactly right, Shane. He's been doing this for ages, I bet! Oh, it makes my blood curdle, thinking of being with him. When we were together, he'd often vanish and miss dates we'd planned. He moves through his women, his conquests and then revisits them, stalks them after it's over. He's even joked about seeing others and how good it was. I could never work out why he'd say this all the time. It wasn't funny but he kept saying it was his joke. But he was obsessed by the prospect ... and toyed with me about it all the time.'

Libby paused, in deep thought, fossicking through what she'd discovered, linking other bits and pieces to complete the puzzle. She was convinced he'd done this before.

'Why? Why does he keep stalking and playing the crack-on game as well? Someone knows, his ex-girlfriends must know because he's such a pro at this. They may know why he moves on too. I bet there are others—all witnesses, all prepared to get him back for what he's done. It can't possibly be just me.'

Shane wondered aloud whether any of these ex-girlfriends, these victims, even if they could be found, would want to revisit the drama. Would they want to dredge up their memories?

'That cop, Haddock, he could find out about the other girls in the police files, right?' Libby said. 'There must be other reports on record. And they could tell me who they are and I can work out the formula, what drives him away, what stops him. He's a professional who's had reason to move on. He couldn't be stalking them all still, otherwise he wouldn't have spent so much time on me.'

If Libby was going to do her own detective work, it had to be done quickly. Her life was in tatters; she felt close to breaking point. She realised that she was on her own and had to take responsibility for her own survival, just as the others would have done. She'd had enough of squatting in a room like a scared kitten, praying for dawn. The time for praying had to end; she had to get her life back—she had to go in search of others like her. If they existed, it was time his victims teamed together. Her desire to stop feeling so alone, so isolated and vulnerable, was motivation in itself to find an ally, even one. She really had no choice. Her life was not hers anymore.

Back at work, Libby spent most of the morning fiddling with the mouse beside her computer, not performing any worthwhile tasks, deep in thought, trying to work out how to approach a stranger, a policeman she'd only known for such a short time. Would he help? Would he be prepared to search for another victim, and was it legal? Libby needed a break, someone to back her case, to help her extricate this creep from her life forever. But she'd only get one shot at recruiting Senior Constable Haddock; she knew she had to be convincing, not a desperate victim who'd become a permanent pain.

Libby dialled the number and asked for Haddock. She had to come clean about what she wanted. The time was right.

'This Phillip Hopkins, who's been scaring the hell out of me for months now, is a professional stalker, Rowan. I know it. He loves these night games. He follows me to all kinds of venues, all different suburbs. I've been to restaurants on the other side of the city and he turned up outside, just to show me that he'd found me. He must have been lurking in the shadows for hours before he decided to show himself. That's complete madness. When we were together, he went missing all the time, no matter how intense our relationship was. He's out there, gathering this captive group of victims. I know it but I can't prove it … and I need your help. I've got no argument without others like me and no way of working out how he can be stopped.'

Rowan Haddock had not heard anything like this before. A stalking case was never easy to prove and, apart from the odd call to police to ward off an aggressive former boyfriend, victims rarely sought their help to investigate further. Very little would eventuate from Libby's two actions before the courts. They both knew this. Rowan would have to bend a rule or two to help, but he knew how he'd feel if he did nothing and Hopkins hurt or even killed Libby. 'I feel for you. I know what you want. I'll see what I can do. If he's had old AVOs against him, the information will be available.'

It didn't take long for Haddock to turn something up. 'You've got a friend out there, Libby,' he told her over the phone the following afternoon. 'You were correct! But you may be shocked at what I've found. There's a woman with a number of AVOs out on him. You've got off lightly. This bloke is dead set crazy. He's not to be trusted, Libby, believe me. He's far more violent than you think.'

Libby wrapped her arms around her chest, as if to brace herself against this new information. She needed to know, but she didn't want to hear it.

'Her name's Simone Crowe. She was a girlfriend too. She's had three AVOs out on Hopkins—three! I don't have the full details, as I can't access the computer, but they're based on at least three serious cases of violence dating back only a couple of years. He bashed this girl over and over again, Libby—and wouldn't leave her alone. It was unrelenting and covered so many years. The sheer number of AVOs tells me that too. He was convicted of assault against her and ten years earlier, as a student, he had similar charges proven.'

Libby went silent. Her body was rigid with anger and aching with empathy for this girl she'd never met. Here was a victim who'd shared her pain. Finally she spoke: 'I should have known; it's been so psychotic. I should have guessed. I could kill him. I've thought about it many times. I just wouldn't know how, wouldn't think I could do it.'

'Stop that talk. Stop telling me that. Stop telling anyone that—it'll get you in trouble. Hopkins needs to be stopped. Just focus on that. Do you want me to find out more? To find Simone?'

'I don't want to get you in trouble. If I wait for the assault case to make it to court, the prosecutors will probably get me this kind of info anyway.'

'Libby, depending on what his lawyers do, that case could be way off. Plus, you'll be lucky to see any detail related to his antecedents, it's classified material ... it's not like the DPP to hand out names and phone numbers. Let me see if I can get a message to her about meeting you.'

Libby knew Simone Crowe would probably want to stay well clear of Libby's case, surely not wishing to talk about it, or replay the drama and dirt over again. But it was worth a shot, Libby thought. It was worth waiting for. So much of her life had been out of her control; she had already displayed more patience than she knew she had.

What an incredible path her life had taken, she thought, ever since that one silly night out on the drink with a girlfriend.

PART TWO: TO TURN BACK TIME

3

HIMBOS AND HIM

'If you can't score tonight Libby, you'd better give up,' Sarah said as the pair stepped up onto the kerb outside the Oaks Hotel.

It was August 1995. Even from here, the girls could hear the hum from inside their occasional Friday-night haunt. Each time one of the doors swung open, the hum became a roar. For the lower North Shore's generation X, the Oaks was the place to be seen.

'I'm not here for that,' Libby replied, as her heels slapped the pavement.

'It's a compliment. You look great,' Sarah said.

Friday night at the Oaks was, for many, a strategic game of sexual energy and dominance. The place was packed with gym-addicted hunks and himbos, whose come-on lines were normally as corny as they were insincere. Genuine, intelligent men rarely approached the girls at this watering hole, but that didn't stop the pair looking; who knows who they'd meet tonight ... maybe Mr Right, probably not. There was no harm in finding a bloke who was fun to be with.

It was the ideal place to find such a man; it was a den of cold beer, sweet wine and wandering eyes. Libby had a model-like figure which most other women envied. Tonight she wore a white blouse and her favourite pair of bottom-hugging jeans. Her long, wavy, white-blonde hair hung over her shoulders attractively; her face was made-up, but not overdone. She didn't need too much; her skin was close to perfect, paler than most, set off by high cheekbones. She'd been told more than once that she had eyes to die for.

Sarah was one of Libby's best mates. Tonight she was happy to let Libby take the lead heading through the frosted doorway at the side entrance to the rowdy pub. Libby ran her fingers through her hair—a last-minute adjustment in preparation for tackling the well-lubricated crowd. She hit the brass doorplate with her open palm and the noise rushed out at them. It now truly felt like Friday night at the Oaks: confronting, noisy, exciting—nothing a few glasses of bubbly couldn't help them take on.

The pair stepped up into the main bar area. There were around a hundred other people aged between sixteen and thirty, mostly standing in groups, drink in hand, gesticulating wildly with each other. Laughter filled their faces. The room was large in comparison to other hotels; the bar hugged the left-hand side, covering a full fifteen metres. Across the other side, a twelve square-metre alcove was jammed with teenagers who looked barely eighteen. It was their hiding spot, away from the scrutiny of the publican and security, but unfortunately within view of entering constabulary. Between the alcove and the centre of the room, scores of drinkers crowded around a series of stools and tables covered in empty glasses and ashtrays and obscured by swaying bodies. Most of the male contingent had come straight from offices in North Sydney, wearing flash business suits that after two and a half hours of drinking time looked noticeably shabby. The decor was a combination of wooden panels and red-striped wallpaper, divided by a shoulder-height wall rail. There were reproduction brass light fittings and picture frames holding black-and-white prints of sporting heroes of yesteryear. The smoky air and loud music kept all this yuppie chaos pumping, despite the fact that it was almost impossible to hear what song was playing.

This, however, was not the area the girls preferred. They needed to push their way through the throng in the centre of the room to reach the courtyard opposite. Pub-shoving was never the most pleasant task for women to attempt; unless, of course, male company escorted them. Libby, hesitated for a second, before she charged into the sea of suits and faces, moving crab-like, her right shoulder braced for the wall of people ahead.

'Excuse me,' she shouted as she shoulder-charged her first victim, her mate tailing her closely.

Before she knew it, a young man had moved aside and Libby found herself surrounded by a group of beer swillers whose conversation had come to an abrupt halt.

'Absolutely, any time love,' one exclaimed.

There were muffled comments, presumably sexual in nature, backed up with approving grunts all round.

'Creeps,' Libby replied quietly, not stopping to survey the circle of gloating faces.

This was normal primitive fare for the Oaks. The two women came to expect it, although they detested the veiled obscenities. They had another fifteen metres to traverse and they picked up speed as they moved, willing their brief pub-shove to end. The next group said nothing, probably because it was a mixed gathering, until Libby's shoulder jolted what looked like a gin and tonic almost out of the hands of one of the women.

'Sorry about that,' Libby said without stopping.

There were dagger stares in return, but Libby gave as good as she got and walked on. She passed two other groups, mostly young men whose tongues were all but touching the floor drooling. They parted as the girls approached but Libby could feel a softly cupped hand brush her jeans as she passed. She stared at the letch for half a second, before pushing his forearm away ... hard. Their stride unbroken, the girls found themselves emerging from the other end of the scrum, through the courtyard door and into the cooler night air. This initial unpleasant Friday-night ritual was over and the night had begun.

'Neanderthals,' Sarah sighed.

'Nothing's changed,' Libby added. 'Don't worry about it. What are you drinking? My shout.'

The Oaks was an interesting division of five different areas, all with their peculiar social groups. While the main bar was where the more uncouth and under-age congregated, a small bar on the other side of the building usually housed older drinkers and had access to betting facilities and cable sports programs. At the other end of the courtyard, a small number of families and a crowd of couples used the under-cover bistro facilities. But the main part of the courtyard was where the cool, well-heeled yuppies gathered. There were around 40 cast-iron tables and chairs, with the bulging oak tree towering over the square. For lighting, a thousand small coloured lights weaved around the branches like a giant octopus, adding a little sophistication to the ambience. Women outnumbered men, but both sexes had plenty of cash, were well-groomed and wore the trendiest gear. It was the closest a pub could get to a nightclub and, like those thumping dungeons, the Oaks was a renowned pick-up-joint for cashed-up young things, most patrons much happier to be picked up by a wealthy, career-orientated looker than by a grungy student in an inner-city nightclub.

Libby and Sarah found a table under the oak. There wasn't really a choice; the pub was packed. They sipped their champagne starters and began chatting about how the week had gone, including which losers at work had been making nuisances of themselves in an effort to attract attention and maybe a date. Libby was a streetwise young woman and was rather choosy as well. All she really wanted was to have a good time with someone she could trust enough to spend a chunk of her currently very laid-back life with. It had been a long time between lovers—although a permanent mate wasn't what she was looking for tonight.

'You're too choosy, you know,' advised Sarah. 'There's nothing wrong with that, but sometimes you've got to take a chance.'

'Maybe,' she said. 'I'm getting so tired of warding off ... ' Suddenly, Libby could feel herself being watched from across the courtyard. A tall guy in his late twenties had set a laser-beam stare on her, but it was his mate who caught Libby's eye. She was now totally distracted. She certainly wasn't listening to anything Sarah was saying. She was looking elsewhere, or more to the point, staring elsewhere.

'Libby?' Sarah said.

Libby was on a different frequency, almost in a trance. About five metres away to her right, in the corner of the courtyard, Phillip Hopkins was listening to what his friend was saying, hardly uttering a word. He was instantly classified as gorgeous by Libby—extremely handsome without being too slick. He wore jeans, boots and white body T-shirt, under a very understated tailored sports jacket. He was well-built, with broad shoulders and a bulky chest. His hair attracted Libby too; deep-brown loose curls, almost black, thick and combed back at the front. It was shiny damp, like he'd just come out of the shower; he looked fresh and clean. As

Libby stared he caught sight of Libby too. He looked up every twenty seconds or so and kept her stare for a while, followed by a shy smile. Those eyes! Libby thought. Now why doesn't someone like that come over to me? 'Sorry, what were you saying,' Libby said.

'You're perving, Libby! You are perving!' said Sarah.

'I might be, but they started it,' Libby said coyly.

Sarah leant over to her right and caught sight of Libby's target. 'He's gorgeous and I think his mate's okay too.'

The pair giggled. Seconds later, Libby's gorgeous man got up and headed towards the bar. Libby was even more impressed. He walked with confidence but didn't appear over-confident; his upper body was strong, obviously a swimmer or an athlete. After he ordered his round of drinks, he looked back directly at Libby and smiled. It was a look Libby was unaccustomed to. The looks she usually attracted at the Oaks were almost sneers. She'd often tell her friends that a particular guy must have thought she was wearing his top. They were nothing more than lecherous perves, uninviting expressions of dominance which Libby loathed. This was very different and exciting. Libby's eyes followed him as he walked back to the table carrying the two drinks. Her heart picked up an extra beat or two.

'What do I do now?' she asked.

'What do you mean? Keep looking on and off. He'll get the hint.'

Libby looked back and the hunk had gone, so had his mate. She frowned, scanning the area. Both girls were turning their heads in all directions.

'Excuse me,' said a male voice from behind Libby.

She was startled and almost lost her balance. As she tried to stop herself from falling over, someone grabbed her chair and interrupted its sway. The hand belonged to the voice, but Libby was in no position to turn and see who it was. Sarah was looking up behind her with her mouth open.

'That was close,' said the voice. 'Sorry about that, I didn't mean to scare you.'

Libby turned a fraction more slowly than she might have. There was no way it could have been the man on her mind. But it was.

'This is going to sound pretty silly, but my friend bet me 50 bucks that I wouldn't come up and ask you if I could buy you a drink. You can split the 50 if you want.'

The girls laughed. True or not, it was a good way to break the ice.

'I don't want to wreck your night, so I'll leave if you like.'

Sarah chipped in: 'Take that other seat.'

'Are you sure? I hate all this "can I buy you a drink" stuff, but I thought it was worth making a fool of myself.'

The girls laughed. Libby still wasn't sure what he was up to, but she was happy enough to find out. One thing she was certain of, those eyes were even better up close. They were soft, blue and tempting. And his face was so finely structured she couldn't take her own eyes off him as he spoke. He even had a dimple.

'While I'm here, my name's Phillip,' he offered.

'I'm Sarah, this is Libby.'

'So, Phillip, what do you do?' Libby asked.

'I'm a computer programmer and kind of trouble shooter in St. Leonards,' he said. 'And you guys?'

'I work up the road at Greenwich with a corporate marketing and production company,' Libby answered.

'In the neighbourhood. A good place to work, isn't it?' Phillip said.

'Yeah, and good for shopping too, which I love,' Libby said.

'True. I shopped for a birthday present for my mum there today.'

It was small talk, but the conversation was drawing them closer. Libby was enjoying their rapport, though she knew it was really nothing more than mutual flirtation—and she was the one doing most of the talking.

Soon enough, Phillip's friend Jason joined them and they had the makings of a party underway. Libby thought the match-up seemed like a damn good idea and proceeded to throw the away rulebook.

'It's my shout; would you like a drink?' she said.

'He looked at her and smiled. Libby slowly climbed off her seat and made her way to the bar. As she waited to be served, she turned and looked at Phillip; he was looking back at her and turned away as if he'd been caught. Libby was convinced this was going to be a great night; the Oaks had something special about it for a change.

Hours passed and the group laughed and joked their way through what seemed like endless rounds of drinks. Everyone had hit the giddy level, everyone except Phillip, who punctuated his bourbons with mineral water. He was clearly still in control and that impressed Libby. She had some experience with heavy-drinking boyfriends and she was always cautious of a man who over-indulged.

The music was belting out at high decibels and each hit was a favourite of one of the groups. Anything from Roachford sent both Libby and Phillip into a frenzy. Soon enough they moved into the main bar where everyone had flocked onto the floor to dance. Phillip and Libby danced only with each other. Their body language said it all. Even the other dancers detected the tactile chemistry between them. At times she put her hands around his shoulders, which were broad, strong and excited her immensely. When he carefully held her around the waist, Libby forgot where her feet were and where they needed to go. She'd forgotten what it felt like to be held, held with passion. She couldn't recall it feeling so good. When Libby went to the bar, Phillip followed. He didn't say much, but wasn't going anywhere.

As the night wore on, their lustful looks and banter intensified. Both were pushing the dare as far as they could. The music seemed hushed and the raucous voices abated. There was nothing except desire. She could see only a divine looking man, whom she knew she could have.

I want him, Libby told herself, as she imagined what his naked body might look like ... how taut his chest might be and how good it would feel to have him caress her all over.

Then, suddenly, the two of them were standing away from the bar, kissing passionately. His arms were wrapped around her body and his fingers were slowly combing her hair. Libby's arms and hands were locked behind his neck. They went from nought to a hundred in a split second. She couldn't get enough of his mouth and each time he forced his hips against hers, she felt a rush of exhilaration. She couldn't recall being so turned on, just from kissing. Then, without warning, he moved his lips away and broke the embrace.

Phillip whispered in her ear, 'I can't get enough of this.'

They kissed for longer, danced more, and laughed at anything that seemed even remotely funny. The excitement of a stranger kissing her felt a little dangerous, but this only fuelled her lust, as did the wine. Should she take him home? Could she even ask the question? Libby would pounce if Phillip asked. The chances that this was a one-night interlude seemed increasingly slim to her. He seemed genuine—in any case, she was hooked.

Suddenly Phillip's attention was completely diverted. He excused himself before approaching the bar and talking to a woman, who he clearly knew. Libby wasn't overly concerned, using the interval to head to the Ladies. She returned to find Phillip still with his friend, close up, in deep conversation. He whispered something in her ear, she kissed him and left without another word spoken. When Phillip returned he told Libby that her name was Frances, a close, old friend. He then changed the subject. Libby wanted to change venue too. She grabbed the others and they headed to the Metropole nightclub in North Sydney, where the four played doubles on the pool tables. A few games, a few more drinks and Libby dragged Phillip away from the sweaty main bar.

As they walked to a quieter side bar to escape the pounding beat of the music, they embraced again. Phillip pulled up a chair, forcefully dragged Libby onto his lap and kissed her wildly. She enjoyed his bold initiative and they pressed hard against each other. Their bodies were primed for sex—and they both knew it.

'This is getting out of control,' Libby said.

'Maybe I should go home,' he whispered, as if testing her attraction.

Libby pulled back, 'Why, what's wrong?'

'Nothing, that's the problem,' he said. 'I don't want to do anything you don't want. You're absolutely gorgeous.'

'You're not going anywhere. Come home with me to Mosman,' Libby whispered as she grabbed his hand and pulled him up off the chair. They were gone.

The journey to Libby's cottage—and her bed—a few kilometres away in up-market Mosman, was a blur. Her bedroom was at the front of the house and the streetlights shone through the wooden slats, spreading striped blue light across the walls and over her bed.

'You look so incredible in the moonlight,' he said. It didn't take long for the real action to begin. Phillip's body was more awesome than Libby had hoped. The lighting flattered his wonderfully proportioned shoulders, biceps and forearms. It had been a long time since she'd had a lover of this calibre in her bed. They made love endlessly, Phillip showing an almost insatiable appetite for sex.

On one occasion he threw her up against wall, lifting her off the floor in the most physical sexual encounter of the night. Throughout this first night, Phillip looked Libby straight in the eye and whispered compliments, telling his new lover how incredible she was. The last thing she could remember was hearing a birdcall in the garden and seeing the tinge of yellow light, piercing through the trees across the street. It was dawn, but she didn't care what time of the day it was, or how much sleep she'd lost.

An hour later, Libby finally awoke and prised her bloodshot eyes open. Staring up at the ceiling, she waved her hand across the sheets to touch him, but no one was there. Phillip had gone without even a note. She jumped out of bed and searched the house, but he was gone and Libby's heart sank. It was too good to be true. He was just like all the others who congregated at the Oaks, a user who only turned on the charm for another one-night stand. How could she have been so stupid?

That afternoon, however, she had little cause to be disappointed. Her home phone rang unexpectedly. Libby wasn't prepared for a call from her new friend. She wasn't even sure how he had found her home number. I must have given it to him, she thought, though she had no recollection of doing so. Either that, or he'd done some quiet detective work of his own on the way out and taken her private number from the telephone dialer. She was now partly relieved, and a little disturbed.

'Hi, it's me,' he said.

'Hi "Me",' Libby replied, secretly happy that Phillip hadn't simply disappeared from her life.

'Sorry I had to take off, but you were fast asleep and probably too exhausted to wake up,'

'I was that,' she replied.

He quickly insisted they meet again that evening, Saturday, and dine out at a fancy restaurant near the beach. Within a couple of hours, Phillip pulled up at Mosman in his shiny Laser and collected Libby like a true gentleman. She was quite impressed.

The pair drove down to Balmoral and, over a candlelight dinner, Libby was about to find out who this new man of hers really was—or so she thought. It was he who seemed to be asking all the questions.

They laughed and chatted about people they admired, common interests they had and music they loved. They'd already discovered they were both into Roachford. Phillip told her how much he loved just staying in and watching a good movie.

'You and I speak the same lingo,' Phillip told her. 'I feel like I've known you for much longer than this.' Libby wanted to be nowhere else; she felt like she was at the centre of the world.

Back at home the lovemaking resumed at full throttle. Twenty-four hours after they first met, the two lovers lay breathless on Libby's lounge room floor, covered in sweat, their bodies entwined and clinging, more from exhaustion than from a need to be close.

'You are incredible,' said Libby breathlessly.

'You are,' he said, as he held her tightly against his body.

It had been a whirlwind introduction. Libby was dazed by the sheer pace of it, shocked by the ease of her own submission, electrified by the breathtaking passion. She wondered whether it was going too fast. She had no idea where this was heading, but she hoped there was much more to come.

On the first Tuesday after they met, they'd arranged to have dinner together. Pick-up was at 7:30pm and Phillip was taking care of everything.

But 7:30 dragged onto 10:30 and it felt even longer. Libby was on the verge of exploding when he eventually arrived—she'd never been kept waiting that long before. As soon as Phillip walked through the door, it was clear he was in a peculiar state of mind.

'Why are you so late?' she asked, trying to calm herself.

'Look I've had a few drinks. I was just really nervous about coming to see you. I'm so sorry.'

Phillip wasn't finished. He told Libby he'd had to leave work later than normal and had then become anxious about her expectations, about having to be the same man as he was when they first met. Strangely, he was giggling through this explanation and Libby knew that he'd had a more than just 'a few'. She asked him to leave. He refused to go until she told him that she understood. She didn't understand and wasn't about to say so. She stood firm and wasn't letting him off the hook. Eventually Phillip left, frustrated and condemned.

The following afternoon he had somehow found her work number and rang her, pleading for her to listen.

At first Libby was adamant that it was as good as over. 'I'm sorry, but that was really strange and I don't think I want to see you again,' she said.

Then Phillip turned on the charm. He told Libby how bedazzled he was with her. In one short phone call he managed to charm his way into her heart, convince her how nervous he had been the previous night. He promised to be the perfect date, given one more chance.

Before the working week was over, Phillip was back in her arms and in her bed, after conjuring up the perfect dinner, a date that featured Phillip asking Libby endless questions throughout the evening. He was besotted too. Or at least it appeared that way. The relationship was back on track after a close-to-perfect evening. The wine dulled any questions that lingered about his behaviour as Libby was swept up in their closeness.

4

ENTWINED

'Dad, Mum, this is Libby. Libby, my dad, Malcolm, my mum, Kathryn.'

'Hello Mr and Mrs Hopkins, nice to meet you both,' Libby said nervously.

'It's Malcolm, Libby, that'll be fine. Okay?'

'Okay.'

Libby was being thrown in at the deep end. Barely a week after meeting a guy in a pub, Libby was sitting in his parents' home, drinking tea in a bone china cup and saucer. She shook her head, wondering whether this was the great idea Phillip had promised it would be. Phillip's sisters and brother arrived at the house at various stages of the afternoon, but the greetings from them weren't so welcoming. One sister not only refused to say hello to Libby, but didn't say more than three words all afternoon. His other sister, who arrived accompanied by her husband, was an angry young woman, who treated her husband like a total doormat. It was set to be an awkward afternoon. I'm meeting the folks in week two. This is crazy, she thought.

She didn't want to spend Sunday alone after such a wonderful, lustful week and Phillip was locked into celebrating his mother's birthday at his parent's house. Libby was curious to see where Phillip had come from though; what his family environment was like and how that fitted with what she'd already seen. She had enormous doubts, however, about going there so soon after they'd met.

The Hopkins' family home was a mansion, with multiple garages, a pool, tennis court and games/gym room, positioned in the corner of a two-acre property. Libby felt she'd been invited onto the set of *Dynasty*, but she wasn't about to tell Phillip that.

'What a great house,' Libby remarked to Phillip when they had a moment alone.

'Mmm, not bad. I'm glad I don't live here anymore though,' Phillip said as he sat down next to Libby on the long leather lounge. 'Dad was driving me mad in the last few years at school.'

'How?'

'Oh, just like Dads do. But mine did it more than others. He wanted me to go to university after doing the private school thing—do law, like my sister, or medicine, like my brother. You know, follow in the footsteps of the rest of the family, build an empire. I just couldn't even think about doing any more serious long-term study. I'd had a gutful. I liked computers; I was good with them and why not do what you like? Dad never approved though, I could tell that …

'Are you hungry? Mum's done the usual over-the-top cooking number.'

'Dinner's on,' called Kathryn from the doorway.

Libby was bustled into the dining room to find a veritable king's feast spread out on the longest table she'd ever seen.

'Oh, that's gorgeous, Phillip. Thank you, darling,' said Kathryn after opening her son's present of perfume.

Libby was taken aback by Kathryn's tone. She spoke to her son as if he were a five year old. Phillip looked at Libby and the pair smiled, recalling their conversation at the Oaks about shopping for her present. But as Kathryn surveyed her gifts, Malcolm diverted their attention away from his wife and onto his own choice of wine.

'Not a bad drop, is it?' he asked.

'No, it's lovely,' Libby replied, feeling a little puzzled that he was ignoring his wife's special moment.

'Dad, hang on. Mum's not finished,' Phillip interjected.

'Oh, come on, she's got a pile of perfume,' he hit back. 'I should know, I've spent a fortune on it.'

Kathryn Hopkins dropped her perfume onto the table, jumped out of her chair and headed quickly for the kitchen, her face turned away. It was clear that Malcolm had a traditional view of a woman's place in the family.

Meanwhile, Phillip had stuck his tongue into his cheek and was looking down at his meal, trying to resist the temptation to correct his father's bad attitude. The tension was bubbling over.

'Nice one,' Phillip said quietly.

'So, Libby, what do you do?' Malcolm asked, as if the past two minutes had never happened.

Malcolm raised his eyebrows at her status as a secretary. She knew what that was about; it had happened from time to time. Kathryn returned a few moments later with coffee and the Hopkins carried on— the perfect hosts. Libby was given a guided tour of the gardens.

She'd made up her mind about Phillip's family; they were certainly a strange lot. His father acted coldly towards him and his mother treated him as no more than a child. As the following hour in their company revealed to her, they were masters of moving on and around unsavoury or confronting subjects. It seemed to Libby that Phillip's father almost considered his son an embarrassment, a drop-out from the old school tie system and the corporate climb that usually followed. Phillip clearly wanted none of that.

'Sorry about my Dad,' Phillip said as they drove home. 'He doesn't have much time for what I do and thinks it's funny to have a go at Mum whenever he wants. But what can I do? I can't chip at him because, every time I try to defend her, he gets even more distant and dismissive. I hate it. He reckons it's his home, his family and I have no right to intrude. When I keep clear of the place, it only hurts Mum. He doesn't allow me to have a key to the house, you know.'

Phillip had more to say about his family. He said that his father had been an affectionate man when Phillip was a child, but had always ruled the house. As his business position had become more elevated, he had less and less time for his son. He recalled going into the study to try and talk to him, to persuade him to play ball games, but his dad had always been too busy. Phillip shared one event with Libby that she immediately understood as an attempt to attract his father's attention. When Phillip was a teenager, he'd gone punk, styling his hair in spikes and dying it purple. When he went to show his father, couped up in his home office,

Malcolm became angry. He yelled at Phillip to get out and told him how embarrassed he was by him.

Phillip also described a rather bizarre evening meal ritual, in which each member of the family would eat separately. As Phillip continued to delve deeper, becoming depressed by his memories of childhood, he spoke of his mother giving him money in secret. If he ran out, she'd top up his bank balance. It wasn't a loan, just a gift to help him out. Phillip's mood had become morbid and, somehow, Libby couldn't quite believe him.

As they approached Mosman, Phillip's ghosts banished, the couple fondled each other. They were becoming a danger to other drivers, as their lust heightened with every passing kilometre.

When Libby found time to catch her breath later that night, she felt content. She was happy to know that the stranger she'd met so recently was no nomad, no evil mystery man. Although her trip to his childhood home had not been without its unanswered questions, he had a solid background, despite his family's dysfunctional behaviour. Nothing she'd seen so far was enough to scare her off. Phillip remained an attractive proposition and she was prepared to give more of herself to her new man. We'll just see how this goes, she thought happily.

Two weeks raced by. All facets of Libby's life seemed infused with an inspiring brilliance. She had endless creative energy at work and her projects seemed to turn out magically well. Phillip showered her with gifts, flowers and small cuddly toys. He even sent her some French perfume, a fragrance Libby had hinted she adored. It was a well-timed extravagance and she enjoyed the fuss.

Sarah thrived on hearing Libby's latest gossip, everything from the magic dating venues to some of the more intimate details that only close girlfriends are privy to. Libby's happiness was limitless. Her parents met Phillip for dinner one night and despite Libby's father's apprehensions, they too began to understand that this man ignited their little girl's life.

One night Phillip invited Libby to a dramatic society play in Chatswood, in which he was playing a major role. In the days leading up to the night of the play, he rehearsed his lines over and over. Libby began to appreciate how much Phillip enjoyed his role as an actor; he loved playing parts and dreaming up ways of portraying someone else. He performed poorly, unable to shake his self-consciousness on stage, but Libby was awfully proud of her new man.

While he had stories to tell Libby about his numerous buddies in the dramatic society, at work and from his old private school, he rarely spent time with them. Jason, from their first night, had since been transferred to Tasmania. Phillip spent almost the whole of his free time with Libby. It seemed a gesture of his commitment.

During week three of their lightning romance, Phillip was holding Libby's hand in one of the back rows at the Cremorne Orpheum cinema. In the middle of a romantic scene, Phillip put his arm around Libby.

'I don't want to scare you, but I think I love you,' he said softly.

Libby froze in her chair, carefully mulling over the correct response to Phillip's bombshell. It's been intense, she thought, but 'love'? Is this good or bad?

Libby had become familiar with Phillip's over-sensitive side and decided to hedge her bets, 'That's so nice.'

Phillip threw his arms around Libby, rubbing her neck, kissing her as though it was their first passionate moment. He seemed thrilled; Libby wasn't sure how to feel and showed it. Phillip paused, looked at her. He could detect her reticence.

Downstairs in the coffee shop, Phillip wanted to take the issue further. 'What's wrong with expressing my feelings to you?' Phillip said, looking agitated. 'What's wrong with that? Are you saying that we have nothing more than a sexual relationship? Are we just friendly? Maybe we should be called friends? Don't you feel strongly for us? Or has love come too early for you? What is it, Libby?'

These rapid-fire questions hit Libby between the eyes. She felt trapped. 'There's nothing wrong with expressing your feelings,' she said slowly. 'And I do feel strongly for you. It's just that, it's just that I guess there's always been an unwritten rule about not "falling in love", as they call it, so quickly. I'm not sure I've ever known what "in love" was.'

Phillip slipped back into the seat of his chair. Libby was perplexed, shocked and scared one moment, guilty at not reciprocating the next.

'Let's go home to your place,' Phillip said as he grabbed her by the hand.

That night, their lovemaking changed. It was more intense than it had ever been. He refused to sleep, appearing to crave an intense, unbroken physical connection.

Later that week, Libby arranged to race home early from work and cook a full-scale candlelight meal. Phillip agreed to arrive at seven-thirty and seemed to be looking forward to experiencing the best of her culinary feats. It certainly promised to be a step up from breakfast and the odd snack. Libby had planned every detail, from serviette rings and candles to the best olive oil and fresh organic vegetables. This was going to be the perfect meal no matter what.

Her modest kitchen bench was in a state of cuisine chaos. Squeezed between the sink and the refrigerator were carefully diced vegetables to serve separately from the pasta dish. She had all the ingredients ready to prepare her Italian bruschetta. A bottle of the best white wine she could find stood in its special wine bucket. She looked a mess but knew she had time to get ready before seven-thirty. As she prepared the meal, Libby put on one of their favourite CDs and rocked along with Roachford in the kitchen.

'Where the hell is he?' Libby said to herself after looking at the hall clock—eight o'clock already. The bruschetta was ready and the fetta was beginning to harden. She couldn't keep it under the grill any longer; the bread was beginning to burn. She rang his flat, but there was no one there; she rang his parents too, but they couldn't shed any light on his whereabouts, and his work extension rang out. Phillip did not like mobiles and claimed hardly to use them outside of work. Libby had never questioned it—she hated them too. He was not contactable and it was now nine-thirty. Every time she heard a car engine outside, she peered out of her bedroom window. She must have looked out the front of the house twenty times to check for him. Then she started to worry.

He'd simply vanished into thin air, so had the pasta sauce in the frypan. The ice had melted under the wine, the rock-hard bruschetta had been tossed into the garbage, the vegetables were dry and tasteless. The entire meal was history. There was no point even beginning to prepare dessert. All that remained was a wonderfully decorated table, sparkling cutlery and her cherished tablecloth. Two stumpy candles were drawing their last breath.

As her eyes welled with tears, she looked down at the table and muttered to herself, 'What an effort, what a waste. Well done, Lib.'

Her concerns for Phillip's safety were disappearing. She sensed she'd been dudded and hated him for it. Libby fell onto the lounge and a dull anger grew in the pit of her stomach, matched only by how sorry she felt for herself. Libby cursed a little further, before falling asleep.

'Call for you, Libby!'
'Who is it, Carla?'
'Phillip again,' said the work receptionist.
'Tell him I'm not here,' Libby yelled back down the office passageway.
'Okay—but this is the very last time.'

It was the morning after the no show and Phillip had already made four calls to Libby's work. She was meting out the first dose of punishment, refusing to take his calls and or to accept the bunch of red roses he sent to her office. Then a letter arrived without a sender's name or address:

Dearest Libby,
   You must be angry and I understand fully. I am so very sorry, so very sorry you'll never know. But you must at least give me the chance to explain. I had one of those nights from hell.

I was dragged off by my supervisor to save a client's mainframe and I was nowhere near a phone and the time just evaporated. The details are way too boring to go into, but I simply had no choice. I thought of you the whole time and by the time I got out of there, it was past midnight and far too late to wake you.

Please forgive me and I promise that it will never happen again. Please call me...

I'll make it up to you. I will.

Love Phillip
xoxoxox

Libby didn't know what to think. It was a plausible excuse, not elaborate enough to be contrived. She rang him at work immediately to apologise for being so cold. They arranged to see each other that night and Phillip brought over a pizza and a bottle of wine for dinner.

'It hurt knowing that you were there on your own with everything prepared, but you have to trust me,' he stressed.

'Well, what was I supposed to think?'

'You should trust me.'

Libby admonished herself for being so quick to mistrust the man she so loved being with.

'I'm sorry,' she said, moving closer to hug him. He didn't say a word, holding her coldly for a few minutes. Then, with no prompting, Phillip was at it again, grabbing at her, tearing her clothing, before throwing her onto the floor and climbing on top of her. She was frightened by his aggression, caught off-guard, unable to calm him down. She felt like a naughty child being spanked for doing something wrong. And for a moment, she believed she deserved it.

5

A PSYCHOTIC MESS

In the week that followed, Phillip rarely stayed at his own apartment at night, becoming a permanent resident at Mosman. While his appetite for sex was as ferocious as ever, he also began experimenting. Libby's limits were about to be tested.

Phillip arrived late one night with a document sachet thick with what Libby presumed was work. But its contents illustrated Phillip's preoccupation with interests well beyond the work sphere. He emptied the sachet and placed a pile of pornographic magazines onto the coffee table. Libby was stunned.

'What are these for'?' Libby demanded.

'What do you think they're for?' he said abruptly.

'Why have you brought them?'

'How about we experiment a bit? You must fantasise about stuff like this, getting dirty. It can make sex even better, you know,' he said. 'Grab us a drink and we'll look through them together.'

'Grab your own drink,' Libby snapped.

'What?' Phillip shouted. 'Don't be such a prude. Lots of couples use this stuff to fire them up or learn something about each other.'

Libby stormed off into the bedroom. Where was his warmth? The magazines were put back into the sachet and never resurfaced again.

On another occasion, while lovemaking, Phillip asked if he could tie Libby up. She was startled, but let Phillip play out his fantasy. She felt very uncomfortable and humiliated—which didn't seem to worry Phillip.

'What was wrong?' Phillip asked afterwards. 'I can't believe you. Let go. I thought this would turn you on.'

'Maybe, but you could tell I wanted you to stop,' she said raising her voice. Libby had dropped the soft and loving tone she'd always used for him. He'd overstepped the mark.

'What do you mean? Did it hurt? I thought you were playing along. I'd never hurt you, baby. I'm so sorry.' Phillip turned away and sounded like he was sobbing. Libby didn't know what to think. It seemed—pathetic. But he sounded so genuinely hurt and, with hindsight, perhaps she could have been clearer about her feelings. Phillip turned back and rested his head on her chest. Libby regretted her outburst, but now she was nursing a sook. Eventually Phillip stood and returned to the lounge room, while Libby sat up on the bed feeling empty and confused.

When he came back into the bedroom, he kissed her on the forehead before making for the front door. Libby asked him to stay, but he walked out and drove away.

Libby headed into the bathroom, turned on the shower taps, undressed and stood under the hot running water. She was grateful for the peace, the space, but why was it so difficult to make her man happy?

Libby Masters was learning the hard way how to deal with a man who possessed apparently boundless sexual energy. He'd connected too deeply for Libby to cut and run. But that didn't mean she was about to run back to him like some punished puppy.

Libby hadn't heard from Phillip for two days; it was the longest period the couple had been apart since they first met. Libby's frustration gnawed at her so much that she could not concentrate at work. On the third night, she rang his apartment at ten o'clock, but there was no answer. Then at eleven, as Libby was in the bathroom brushing her teeth before bed, she was startled by a loud knock at the door.

'Who is it?' Libby yelled down the hall. There was no answer. 'Is anyone there?'

There was still no answer. She was becoming frightened. Someone had been there for sure. If it was Phillip, he would have answered by now.

She returned to the bathroom and she could see a tiny silhouette through the small bathroom window out onto the backyard. The shadow grew larger. Her heartbeat raced. Then in a second the silhouette became the clear full shape of a person, followed by a rap on the sill. The fright made Libby drop the glass of water she had been holding and it smashed onto the cold, tiled floor.

'Who is that?' she screamed.

'It's me,' Phillip replied. 'Sorry, there was no answer out front.'

'Oh,' Libby shut her eyes with relief and sighed, going to the back door to let him in.

'Did I scare you?' Phillip asked blankly.

'You sure did,' Libby said, holding her chest. 'Didn't you hear me yell out down the hall?'

'No. I decided to go round the back. I must have been round the side when you yelled.'

'How have you been?' Libby asked as she took a dustpan and broom from behind the door and headed back towards the bathroom to clean up.

'Oh, okay, and you?' Phillip followed from a distance.

Libby came out from the bathroom and took a good look at him. He sounded over-excited, tense. His face was flushed, as if he had a fever. Libby couldn't understand why. He has a car, she thought. He didn't run here.

'I've got something for you,' Phillip said, as he stood alone in the lounge room, following her movements with his eyes.

He took a videocassette out from under his dark grey sloppy joe and made his way to the video recorder in the lounge room, inserting the cartridge into the machine.

'What's this?' Libby asked curiously, as she returned to sit down on the lounge. 'We're not watching a video are we? It's eleven o'clock, Phillip, and I've got an early start tomorrow.'

Phillip hopped back onto the lounge as saxophone music blared from the television screen. A grainy picture appeared, a wide shot of a park. The camera began to zoom in and Libby could see what she was watching. A man with messy, blonde-streaked hair was having sex with a breast-enhanced woman on a picnic bench. The music was mixed with overacted groans and grunts. Although she winced in disgust, Libby was conscious not to overreact and trigger another argument over a videotape. She stayed put to watch, until after ten minutes she'd had enough and went to bed. Phillip, however, ignored her walkout and stayed up to watch the rest of the tape alone.

Deep down Libby was genuinely fearful that Phillip Hopkins was attempting to orchestrate what they did without any kind of consultation. Was he just a little insecure in this new relationship? Or was there something more sinister behind his behaviour?

Libby needed her friends around her again. Her helter-skelter time with Phillip was making her feel a little suffocated. She threw a small dinner party. Sarah came along, as did Libby's sister Anna, who had a family of her own and didn't get together with the girls too often. Good food and good wine were the order of the night—with a dash of good humour. In fact, as the night rolled on, they became a cackling and raucous trio, making fun of anyone they could think of, including Libby's new boy.

'You should see him eat!' said Libby.

'Yeah anyone who's been cavorting in the bedroom as much as you reckon he has must have a huge appetite,' said Sarah.

The girls laughed loudly.

'No, I mean you should really see him eat; he has gross manners, atrocious manners!'

At that, Anna almost lost her entire mouthful of red, spluttering it across the dining room table.

'He's a bit of a boy then, is he?' asked Sarah.

'A bit of a boy? You're kidding. He looks like a Neanderthal when he's in full swing—just awful!' she said.

'No!' said Anna shocked. 'You can't have that ... I thought he went to a private school and came from a respected family. What do you mean?'

'He's just a pig really. I have a go at him, but he forgets and goes back to his lazy ways, chewing with his mouth open. It's appalling,' said Libby.

The women laughed until their sides ached. Libby was just playing, but it was true that Phillip did indeed have terrible manners.

The following afternoon, Phillip enticed Libby to take a long drive out of the city. 'When was the last time you had sex in a car?' Phillip asked as they drove. This was a little more familiar territory for Libby, who had spent plenty of evenings as a teenager in her boyfriend's snazzy new car.

'A long time ago, probably thirteen years ago,' she said. 'A wham-bam-thank you ma'am, really. He was so nervous; it was over in fifteen seconds.'

Libby found the recollection funny. Phillip was stony-faced. 'I didn't ask for the details, just when,' he said abruptly. 'By the way, do you really detest my table manners?'

Libby froze. How could he have known what she'd said, unless he heard her conversation with the girls the other night?

'How do you know that?' Libby asked.

'Oh, I just know it. I hate being humiliated ... when it's not true either.'

'You've picked up on some conversation somewhere, have you?'

'Might have ... might not have. What conversation are you talking about?'

'Oh stop it. You heard us girls having fun the other night. Just playing we were. But you heard that. How? Were you snooping outside the house?'

'Not snooping. I came over the other night. I thought I'd left my wallet there and before I could knock, I heard you embarrassing me. How horrible is it to eat with someone who has such bad manners, hey?'

'It was a joke. And anyway, you know you lapse sometimes, Phillip.'

'It was bloody awful of you to say that. Why would you hurt me like that? I didn't knock. Of course I didn't knock. I listened and left ... and found my wallet the next day.'

'Bullshit, you must have been listening from the back window. We were in the kitchen, around the dining room table. You couldn't have heard us from that far away. Why lie?'

'You were yelling, obviously after having too much grog,' Phillip said aggressively. 'I could hear you clearly from the front door. Don't make it out to be anything else. This is your stuff-up, not mine.'

Libby didn't bite back, partly because she wasn't sure how loud the three of them had actually been. But she was starting to become somewhat curious at Phillip's strange predilection for lurking in the shadows of her home.

They made no contact with each other for almost a week. This was a stand-off and neither was prepared to break the ice. In fact in the first few days, Libby considered the relationship to be over, but as the days passed, she inexplicably began missing the side of Phillip she liked most.

For now, there was no way she was about to provide her friends with a commentary on her tawdry relationship. She so wanted to tell someone what was going on, but her life was in a state of confusion. They were very lonely days and her old warm feelings for Phillip kept resurfacing. The more she replayed recent events, the more her mind played tricks on her, the more she began blaming herself.

Maybe this was her problem. Yes, Phillip's obsessions were a little perverse but, as her anger subsided, she reminded herself of his kindness and ability to be soft and loving. She couldn't understand why he became distracted so often. She was prepared to accept that she did really want the old Phillip back but wasn't sure whether he was capable of relinquishing some of his obsessive behaviour. She had to confide in someone. Her soul was bursting. Eventually she broke. 'Maybe he had a bad childhood,' she told Sarah. 'He told me once that his previous girlfriends simply accepted all that hyped-up sexual stuff and loved it. What do I do?'

'You've got to talk to him, Libby,' Sarah instructed during lunch. 'Get him on neutral ground and tell him exactly what you'll accept and what you won't. That's, of course, if you want him back.'

'I think I do. It's weird, I'm almost prepared to walk away, but I feel as if I should give him another chance.'

That afternoon, following lunch with Sarah, an envelope sat in her pigeonhole at work. She took it back to her desk to read it, hoping it was from Phillip:

Libby,

Please accept my apology. I've stuffed up. You've seen my faults first hand and you hate me, I can feel it.

I've done a lot of thinking in the past week though. I apologise for every knee-jerk pathetic reaction ... it's happening too much, I know. My heart is with you though, and you only. You know that don't you? In your heart of hearts.

I keep pushing too hard, trying to push you into things that are not you. I'm still scared that one day it's going to be too good! But I look forward to it.

I desperately want you back. You can initiate anything from here. I'll do what you want. You take the lead, as you said you wanted to.

I miss you so much. I miss your wonderful body too ... Please call me.

I LOVE YOU ...

Phillip
xoxoxox

His words almost brought Libby to tears. He was so honest and open about his own frailties. And his desire to be with her and her alone was palpable. How did we get to this point, she thought to herself? This stuff he's 'into' is not kinky, it's just a little daring and voyeuristic. She still knew that his ideas might not be for her, but she recognised then that she needed to 'get over it'.

She called him later that afternoon and they met that night. There were very few words, very little ironing out of the problems that stood between them. After being so close, then so apart, their lust for each other overcame all. They made love like they used to, over and over again; all their anxieties and frustrations were channelled into physical affection. Phillip was less aggressive now, and her fragility made her melt in his arms again.

The following day Libby and Phillip met for lunch at a quaint sandstone cottage restaurant. It was a special day, filled with all the laughter and magic of old. They joked about being sacked for returning to work late and held hands across the table, barely aware that the restaurant staff were waiting for them to leave. Phillip escorted her all the way back to her office, kissing her passionately in front of Libby's colleagues in the foyer. Her female workmates were green with envy, her male colleagues wide-eyed. They'd never seen this side of Libby Masters before.

In the week that followed, things were to change dramatically. On one particular night, Phillip turned up two hours late for a home-cooked dinner at Libby's house. It was not to be the only time he missed a scheduled rendezvous. His calls were infrequent and he was decidedly quiet. He didn't stay over as he had previously, opting to spend the night at his own apartment instead. Phillip explained that he had embarked on a fitness campaign that meant rising at five in the morning and either swimming or riding a bike until eight-thirty. He was exhausted and apologised for being forgetful and late.

His erratic behaviour was surfacing more than ever too. On one occasion, as the couple travelled over the Harbour Bridge, fuelled by alcohol he threw a two dollar coin directly at the toll collector's face. He laughed like a maniac and made racist remarks about the Asian toll collector as he drove away. Libby didn't know what was happening to him—and she could smell a rat about his time away from her.

'What do I do, Sarah?' she asked over lunch one day. 'I confront him and he seems to have an excuse. But I know something's wrong. He's even avoiding staying and having sex with me.'

'What?' Sarah said, surprised, considering the wild stories she'd been told previously.

'Maybe there's someone else,' Libby said, finding it hard to look up from the table. 'There could be. You know the signs. They don't care much, they're always late and sex virtually evaporates.'

'Test him out,' Sarah said.

She could make him jealous by avoiding him, blaming her busy schedule. They hatched a plot for him to spot her at the Oaks and she would, if necessary, clearly flirt with someone else. Phillip would probably be curious enough to turn up and check out what they were up to. He wore his jealousy on his sleeve. They agreed that Phillip needed a jolt to test his commitment.

The plan was carried out to the letter. Libby told Phillip she couldn't see him the following Friday night because she was going out to the Oaks with Sarah. He asked why, but didn't persist when Libby explained that she'd planned it for a while and felt bad about ignoring her best friend for so long. She went out and the girls caught up with some old friends, schoolmates too, who she hadn't seen for quite a while. Dancing late that night, Libby's male friends guided her around the dance-floor arm in arm, bouncing hips playfully. Through the crowd of heads and shoulders she occasionally glanced around to see if she could spot Phillip watching from beyond the dance floor. But neither of the girls saw him anywhere that night.

It was Sunday before Libby heard from Phillip again. Around mid-afternoon she heard an aggressive knock at the door and went up the corridor to answer it. 'Who is it?' she asked.

'Me,' came Phillip's stern reply.

As soon as she unlocked the door, it burst open, throwing her back against the wall. Phillip stormed in without any thought for what damage the flying door may have done. His face was red with rage, his stride long as he made his way down the corridor and into the lounge room.

'What the bloody hell do you think you're doing, Libby?' Phillip screamed. 'A night out with the girls, huh? Getting touched up by horny pisspots and acting like a tart. You've embarrassed me again, made me look like a dickhead. Why hurt me like that?'

'What are you talking about? Did you turn up at the Oaks?' Libby replied softly.

'A minute was all I needed, yes,' he said.

Then Phillip went berserk, throwing his car keys across the room, going to hit the television set. He kicked a terracotta plant pot and it rolled over, spilling the plant across the mat and crashing against the fireplace. He pushed the lounge out of its position. He then strode up to within a few centimetres of Libby and began a verbal tirade that would have been heard next door.

'What have I done to you of late that made you do this?' he said, screwing his face up with anger. 'I've dropped all the stuff that you hate. I buy you dinner when I can, work out to keep myself fit, tell all my friends what a wonderful chick you are—and you do that to me. You chuck it back in my face.'

Libby was trembling, not knowing how to explain what she'd set out to do, not daring to reveal that it was a plan to win him back.

'I just—' she paused.

'You just bloody what? What?'

'I thought you were seeing someone else,' Libby mumbled.

'What?' he screamed. 'Seeing who? Why would I do that? That's the most idiotic thing I've heard. Can't you understand that I'm flat out at work and trying to do a hundred things at once? Maybe I'd better get to it so you can go on with this crazy crap with someone else.'

'No, I don't want that.'

Phillip was still yelling, his hands still flying. Then as he launched into another tirade, his right hand clipped Libby's chin, knocking her almost off her feet.

'Oh! I'm sorry,' Phillip said, leaning over her to see what he'd done. 'I'm sorry. I didn't mean it, I promise. I just go crazy when it all stuffs up on me again.'

He had broken the skin and the sight made him fret. Phillip ran into the bathroom and returned with a wet hand towel, attempting to stop the blood.

'I'm sorry too, Phillip, I was stupid,' she said.

Libby reached up to hug him. They held each other tight. She felt a great sense of relief, not because they'd come to any resolution, but because the rage was over. If the situation required pretence, Libby was up to it; anything to prevent a repeat of what she'd just witnessed.

Something else bothered her too. Libby could smell a familiar perfume on Phillip, a recognisable aroma. In fact, she believed it was the same fragrance he'd given to her. Her suspicions about Phillip's extra-curricular activities were now as good as proven. Perhaps he even bought different women the same perfume to prevent suspicion. The pieces were starting to fall into place. Phillip Hopkins was a fraud; a dangerous fraud.

As Phillip switched off the lounge room light, gesturing towards the bedroom, she closed her eyes. She felt like crying as he led her there. In bed, engulfed by repulsion for the man treating himself to her body, Libby could only console herself with one fact: this would be the last time, the very last. After that, it was time to find somewhere to hide.

6

IGNITING EVIL

'Are you sure he's that screwed up?' asked Sarah, as Libby took a nervous sip of her coffee.

The pair had met at Libby's insistence during their morning tea break and Sarah sensed she'd been summoned to a crisis meeting.

'You just heard it all.' Libby said forcefully. 'I can't take it anymore, not for another second. We're arguing all the time now. You don't know him. He's a real little bastard, a spoilt little child. If he doesn't get his way, he gets so rude, so cruel.'

If Sarah was honest, she'd known worse. She'd been through the dirty magazine and porno movie trip with more than one of her own boyfriends. She'd also met men who were totally unrealistic in their expectations.

'I hope you know what you're doing,' Sarah warned.

'You don't have to cope with his childish obsessions, his ego and his demands that everything goes his way,' Libby insisted, as she stood to leave.

She wasn't as certain as she sounded. She could still feel his touch, hear his kind voice and see his smiling face. Nothing made sense.

'You've got to end it, if that's what your heart says,' Libby's mother concluded, after hearing the censored version of her daughter's plight.

Libby was convinced, even if she hadn't worked out the best approach. There was an added complexity in that his birthday fell the following day. Still, this had to be the end.

'Phillip's on line three, Libby,' Carla told her through the speakerphone.

'He's done it again!' Libby exclaimed. Phillip had cornered her in another moment of uncertainty. It was as if he could sense the storm clouds between them and had to get in and fix things before they broke.

'Hi,' Libby said cautiously.

'Hi. I've missed you,' Phillip replied. 'A lot.'

'Listen, Phillip, we need to talk,' she interrupted.

'Talk? What do you mean "talk"? That sounds ominous.'

'Can we meet, maybe tomorrow night?'

'Nice of you to remember my birthday. I'll pick you up at eight. I know a good place.'

'Okay, it doesn't matter where, I'll see you then,' Libby interrupted again, before hanging up.

This was not going to be easy. It was risky to end it in her home; there was no telling how he'd take it. Would he explode again? Or could he see the writing on the wall and be resigned to the news? Even if he knew it had to end, he would probably sob like a baby, one of his usual attention-seeking methods. She was not certain he'd remain calm even in public.

Libby parked her car in the driveway of her home after returning from some late afternoon shopping and walked the path to her front door. It was just on sunset, dark enough for the streetlight to be on: it shone a dim beam on her front yard. As she approached the door, she began scrambling for her keys; they were tangled at the bottom of her bag. She fiddled for the key ring, trying repeatedly to untangle the keys.

As she did so, a hand appeared in front of her and thrust a set of keys in her face. She jumped in fright. The hand, dangling the keys arrogantly on the forefinger, belonged to Phillip.

'Use mine,' he said smiling, hand outstretched.

'You scared me, you bastard!' Libby shouted. 'Are they keys to my front door?'

'Well, yeah,' he admitted.

'How did you get them?'

'That's a secret,' he replied smugly. 'Aren't you going to wish me happy birthday?'

Libby was now in no mood to interrogate him further. Having keys cut was brazen and invasive, but she had a greater priority on her mind. After dropping her shopping bags on the lounge, she freshened up in the bathroom and herded him out the door again. There was little point in drawing the night out.

They went to dinner at a local BYO, then for a drink at a bar. All the while, Libby was distant and distracted. She couldn't pick the right time to let Phillip down easily. No moment seemed right. By the time they returned to Libby's place, it was after midnight and Phillip went straight to the bedroom, clearly expecting that Libby would follow him.

Hardly a word was spoken. Libby stalled, moving washing baskets, picking up clothes, spending forever in the bathroom, tidying the kitchen—anything but heading into the bedroom. He called her to come in five times. Eventually she replied, 'No, not tonight. I'm not interested.'

As she leant down to pick up a pillow from the lounge room floor, Phillip came up to her from behind and went to grab her shoulders. She moved her elbows up to stop him touching her and the mood was now set. 'You know what I'm going to say, don't you?' Libby said, standing near the fireplace with her arms folded across her chest.

'No. You've got the shits I know that.' Phillip sat back into the lounge. 'If it's still about me scaring you, I'm sorry, it's one of my bad habits. I won't do it again. And the keys, I thought it might have been handy if I had a set.'

'Stop it. It's no good anymore. I don't know whether I believe you. I don't know whether you're having me on, or not having me on … I'm so confused and I can't cope anymore. Do you understand?'

Phillip stood from the lounge as if to offer reassurance and Libby immediately took a step back.

'Don't,' she warned. 'Just sit down, I haven't finished. You've hurt me Phillip, emotionally and physically. You're so unpredictable—you scare me. I know you've got some problems, you know, childhood stuff that won't go away … I understand that, I've tried to excuse you because of it. You're obsessive. You seem unable to accept the word 'no', or not having what you want. I've had enough. I want to end it. I want to end it now.'

She said it. She finally said what she'd been wanting but also fearing to say for days. Libby could feel the physical relief, the heavy weight lift off her shoulders, but she was shaking, waiting for Phillip's reaction.

'Okay. I got all that,' Phillip said, unusually quietly. 'I can see that you mean it. You're truly over us, aren't you?'

Libby nodded but said nothing. Phillip stood up and moved over towards the kitchen doorway. 'I'm not walking out of here without putting a few things straight—things that you've completely misconstrued, totally misconstrued. That's what you've done. You know as well as I do that you can't handle love. All that independent woman junk you chicks believe, it's just an excuse you use to get laid, to get laid by as many men as you can. I've only wanted to please you, be with you, and you turn me away.'

Phillip's voice was raised now. He was sobbing and she knew he was going for the emotional jugular. She was trying desperately not to crack. Phillip moved closer to her. 'Do you realise what you've done, Libby?' he shouted. 'You've taken me for a ride all this time. You've toyed with me and then when the heat turns up, you walk.' He was pointing into Libby's face, his voice growing louder. 'Don't you dare blame me for hurting you, scaring you,' he yelled. 'You're the one who's become an expert at that cruel game. You are a loser ... you've lost someone who cares, who could be your soul mate. You're the scary one, not me.'

Libby began to cry, overcome. Phillip grabbed her by the arms with great force and shook her. 'Can't you see?' he yelled. 'You've crushed me, again. First it was the flirting, the jealousy ploy; now let's make Phillip grovel. Not this time, not on my bloody birthday!'

With that, Phillip threw his hands wildly in the air and his arm clipped an ornament on the mantlepiece. It hurtled to the ground and smashed into pieces on the floorboards. He was in an emotional frenzy, yelling, ranting, pleading. He stormed around the room, smashing his fists into walls, before breaking down in hysterical tears. The whites of his eyes were almost purple and he stared straight through Libby. Then, he spat at her; a foul glob of mucous splattered across her cheek and mouth.

She was totally repulsed and sickened. Her legs trembled, her heart was pounding violently and she feared for what else he was about to do.

She made for the bedroom, totally distraught. Phillip tried to grab her shoulder as she turned, but managed only to catch her dress from behind, ripping it down the side. She pulled away, lengthening the tear.

'Get out! Get out of here now!' she screamed, backing away.

He wasn't in the mood for taking orders. He followed her into the bedroom and grabbed her again, throwing her onto the bed. He tried to put his hand over her mouth but she managed to squirm out of his hold and away from his hand. She screamed as loudly as she could. It was deafening—Phillip retreated from the bed, then abruptly left, slamming the front door. Libby lay perfectly still, heart pounding furiously. What would he do now? Would he actually leave?

After ten silent minutes, she was convinced he'd truly left. She changed, throwing the ripped dress in the bin before turning most of the lights out. She curled up in bed in a state of sheer exhaustion. Her head was pounding, her eyes stinging and she just wanted to sleep. But as she closed her lids, she heard a muffled knock at the window to the kitchen. It came again and she tentatively made her way down the corridor. As she stood silently in the darkened kitchen, the front door suddenly flew open and there was Phillip, standing in the shadows, waiting for a reaction. 'I want to talk to you,' he said quietly.

'I don't. Get out. Get out now.' She stepped across to the telephone, picking it up. 'I'm calling the police, Phillip. I'm not mucking around any more.'

Phillip walked into the house and stood in the kitchen, pleading for Libby to listen to him.

'Don't do this. Listen to me, I can't handle this.'

He had only one avenue left to turn her around. He needed to seek sympathy before she made that call, before she wiped him from her life forever. It was obviously unacceptable. He seemed intent on doing everything possible to change that, as he meandered through his good points, the failings he needed her help with and the pointlessness of a life without her.

'I'm weak without you. I need you, Libby. I know that now.'

When that fell on deaf ears, he yelled and screamed in rage.

'I'll be out the front,' Libby told the emergency operator and left through the front door to wait for the police. She moved right out onto the footpath, a few metres from her front gate. Phillip moved up behind her silently; she was unaware of his presence until it was too late. He grabbed her arm and hair and threw her onto the nature strip. 'You bitch!' he yelled. 'This ain't going to happen!'

Before he could get hold of her on the ground, Libby scrambled to her feet and began to run. Hopkins was right behind her. 'Where are you going, Libby? You can't run from me. You want to end it now do you? Well that's not going to happen. You are mine.'

He was right; she couldn't get away. It was hopeless. 'Stop it … please?' she begged.

He was quiet now, for fear of alerting the neighbours, but lights around them were already coming on. He grabbed her by the hair and began dragging her up a nearby street, a lane with no lighting. The rough surface of the path and the gravel of the driveways ripped the skin on her back as he dragged her 50 metres up the lane. She tried regaining her feet but he was moving too fast. His eyes were enraged. Whatever torture he was about to inflict upon her, Libby was powerless to stop him.

Then she heard two or three men yelling from down the lane.

'Hoy, let her go!'

'Hey, what do you think you're doing, you bastard?' another shouted.

Phillip dropped her on the ground and her shoulders hit the kerb painfully. He disappeared along the lane and then she heard the sound of sirens approaching. Libby was battered and bruised but able to stand.

Within a minute, one police officer was asking her how she was and placing his hand around her shoulder, as another spoke briefly to a frantic neighbour in a dressing-gown outside her house. They had caught Hopkins, the officer told her, and he was being taken away.

Libby was escorted back to her house—it looked like a crime scene. She didn't want to be there anymore.

The police took Libby to her parents' house that night, where she spent all of the next morning, Sunday, recovering from her ordeal. Her first verbal contact was with the constable who handled the night's drama and had processed Hopkins at the local police station. He rang to inform her that the Hopkins' family had posted bail and he'd been released. The officer was certain Hopkins had experienced his own ordeal and would not return to frighten or threaten her, at least not in the short term.

Later that afternoon, Libby's sister arrived to help out. They agreed to go back to Mosman to collect more of her clothes and personal items. As they drove to the top of her parent's street, Libby immediately spotted Phillip's bright red Laser and he was sitting behind the wheel. As they passed he started his car and began to tail Libby and her sister from two car lengths behind. They managed to lose him in traffic, but Libby refused to go home. She stayed the night at her sister's and there was no further sign of him that weekend, but Libby remained unsettled.

Over the next few days, as Libby returned to work, against all advice, Phillip appeared at every turn. When she got off the bus, he stood opposite the bus stop for a few moments. When she reached her office, Phillip emerged from around the corner. If she was alone, he'd launch a pathetic appeal.

'You're making things worse and I wish you'd just go away,' she said.

'But I love you, I can't live without you Libby.' This was his constant lament.

Depending on who else was around, he would even follow her into her security-controlled building. He stood next to Libby as she tried to swipe her card to get inside and wouldn't budge, pleading with her hysterically. He kept this up until he thought someone was coming. Once he managed to force his way into the foyer. When a colleague went to exit, Libby used the opportunity to push him back out the door just before it closed.

From outside the building, he hassled Libby with flowers and notes begging for forgiveness. When Libby caught the bus home, Phillip would pull up in his car at her stop and drive alongside her at walking pace with the window down to plead some more.

'I'll kill myself Libby—I will,' he yelled out of the car. Libby walked undeterred and seemingly unaffected. He eventually drove away at speed, angry and distraught.

Then there were the painful letters, personally delivered, sometimes two on the same day. On 13 December he wrote:

Libby,

I can't function without you—I can't think, eat or sleep unless drugged. My life isn't here anymore. You're my life. The pain is persistent and unbearable. I miss you. I miss seeing you, talking with you every day—that's why I need to see you, and why I have done what I have done. Not to hassle you or assault you or even to be a nuisance. Just to receive this pain. If you believe that, then there is no need to call the police again. That would kill me and nothing I have done deserves that, does it? And honestly, Mum would be affected severely as well. Please don't.

I miss your beautiful face, with your hair out and over your shoulders, looking down on me lovingly, touching me. Me touching you.

Libby, you are pushing me out—and I told you that is what you must do if you want to end our relationship—and not build it up into something so strong no one or nothing can beat it. If that's what you want you will have to keep on doing so until I give up hope. I don't know how long that will take. Don't worry, I won't see you persistently or call you or see you in front of anyone concerned about you. But when I give up hope I'll stop.

But I will always love you. And always, anytime soon, you can call me and maybe we can talk. In time, you will have someone else and I will too—and our good times will be remembered and what might have been will be wasted.

Please call me, Please see me.

I love you. That's all that counts.

Going home from work became a tactical attempt to avoid him and keep as close as possible to others. One afternoon she walked down the fire stairs with a colleague and Phillip was there, but continued past the pair, as if too afraid to confront her in the company of an unknown entity. At the bus stop, he arrived from nowhere again. 'I love you, I cannot live without you,' he said.

At that moment, her colleague Carla, also leaving work, spotted Libby being hassled by the man she'd noticed lurking around the building. She screeched to a halt at the bus stop and opened the passenger door. Libby instantly ran over and hopped in.

Libby spent another night in the spare room of her sister's house, but she knew it was only a matter of time before he'd turn up there too. She was now at her wit's end. He returned to her workplace the following day and managed to get inside the building yet again.

'That's it, Phillip,' she said forcefully. 'I know you're upset. I was prepared to allow you that grief until now. Enough! I will ring the police again and you'll be in deeper trouble. Go away.'

Only the appearance of a stranger forced him to turn and leave.

That lunchtime, he was up the road, trying to intercept her walk to the shops. Libby wondered whether he actually spent any time at work. She turned to walk back to her building, shattered by the realisation that this was not going to end any time soon.

As she reached her office block, a hand grabbed her wrist from behind. His face was filled with rage. He began pulling Libby towards his car at the kerb. Two colleagues came running out of the security doors and broke the lock he had on her wrists. He jumped in his car and screeched away.

Within 30 minutes of this incident, after Libby had spent some time tidying herself up in the washroom, she returned to her desk to find yet a letter—another warning that he couldn't live without her.

She could no longer cope with the constant onslaught. Three days after Phillip's vicious assault, she called the police once. Her friend Shane agreed to take her home to collect her belongings. She was now on leave from work.

As Shane drove Libby out from the underground carpark and onto the Pacific Highway, Hopkins was close by, leaning against a wall. Spotting her in the passenger's seat, he stepped towards the passing car and mouthed a message to her: 'Don't ring the police.' But it was too late. They were on their way.

At that moment though, Libby no longer cared whether the police would catch him, or what they would do to him. She simply longed to be safe, to escape to a new place; a place Hopkins would never have conceived she'd go.

7

BASHED

'You can stay here as long as you like, Libby,' called the reassuring voice from the other room.

She was simply too petrified to stay alone. Overnight her home in Mosman had transformed into a cold, heartless shell. And it wasn't only her cottage that felt unsafe. Phillip Hopkins had proved that he could track her down almost anywhere. No reassurance from the police could convince her otherwise. Yes, he now had a court-case to front after Christmas, the further allegations of force and constant harassment to defend, but his family had money. Libby had read enough to know that crimes of passion were often treated sympathetically by courts. And she was now smack bang in the middle of one of those stories that up to now she'd only read about.

She longed for solitude and needed rest, but for now she also had to keep well clear of her parents' home and her sister's too. All connections had to be broken. Phillip didn't know about her friend Anthony in Melbourne. They had not been together long enough to travel there together. She just hoped that Phillip hadn't followed her to the airport—or even to Melbourne—but she couldn't be entirely sure. Anyone who'd been through what Libby had of late had every reason to keep looking over their shoulder, even so many hundreds of kilometres away from home.

As far as her stalker was concerned, Libby had simply vanished from the face of the earth. She spent most of her days holed up in Anthony's small lounge room and on the even smaller apartment veranda overlooking the postage stamp-sized park below. South Yarra felt a world away from her life on Sydney's warm north shore.

Anthony was a former beau—very former—and was the only person in Libby's life detached from her current set of friends. He no longer held any attraction for Libby—although the fact that he lived so close to the Toorak Road shopping strip was a pleasant distraction. The upmarket boutiques and the cafés slowly lured her out of the apartment and elevated her soul. Anthony was extremely busy and not often able to entertain his interstate guest, but that was exactly what Libby needed, solitude and an environment conducive to mental rehabilitation. Most of all, she felt safe.

Libby felt empowered by her isolation, stronger in mind and spirit. The quiet apartment block, the serene park below and all those scarfed Melbournians going about their business felt so far away from the maddening captivity she'd been living in. Anthony didn't ask too many questions about the condition she was in. He knew what had happened that night and during the days afterwards, but little about what had led up to these events. He'd known Libby long enough and intimately enough not to push her towards breaking point. She was slowly letting her guard down, revealing bits and pieces of the story, but it would happen in her own time.

The Libby Masters Anthony had known had everything going for her. Even now, under duress, she was a very beautiful young woman. Her face and eyes were kind and warm, her complexion pale and close to perfect, her hair long, wavy and blonde. Many a discerning man had become mesmerised by that girl-next-door look. Her figure was exceptional, the envy of her workmates and girlfriends. And her career had been going well too. Her hours were flexible, she got out and about quite often and she worked in an interesting industry.

However, at this point in her life, not surprisingly, Libby was a troubled soul and she had some important decisions to make. She knew she couldn't hide indefinitely, that she needed to take affirmative action. Her week interstate was a wonderful tonic, but it would soon be time to return home. She wasn't sure whether she'd see Anthony again. He'd clearly moved on with his life. Perhaps she was on the brink of doing the same. In an emotional farewell, they agreed to keep in contact and Anthony told her that he hoped her troubles would soon be over.

Back home, having found solace in the company of a male friend, Libby wanted to protect herself in a similar way. Her psyche craved a bodyguard. She recruited Shane, who had always been there for her when she needed advice from a man. Theirs had been a relationship at arm's length—strictly platonic, on her part at least—but he was up to speed on Libby's troubles and he only had to peer into those once soft and beautiful eyes to see the terror and despair that had engulfed her life. He'd given his two cents' worth on several occasions already, even encouraging her to take the trip to Melbourne. He was happy to assist in any way possible and readily agreed when she suggested they go out to dinner together.

Libby dropped into Mosman on her way to the Manly café where she'd planned to meet Shane for an early Saturday night meal. Her home seemed so creepy and daunting now; pangs of fear crept back into her stomach as she walked shakily up the hallway and into her bedroom. Her neck was stiff with tension as she swapped her soiled casuals for her favourite blouse and jeans. Her movements couldn't have been any faster. Her stop off lasted only a few minutes, but it was a cold return to the home she'd once loved. As she left she opened the letterbox to find yet another of Phillip Hopkins' apologies, another plea for them to be together again. This time the package had a cassette enclosed:

Libby,
I've enclosed a cassette of songs as a gift to you with a couple of songs that describe how much you mean to me ... if you listen to the lyrics, they describe my feelings—which I have so much needed to communicate to you over the past couple of weeks. I've included 'our' song, Roachford's 'Only to Be With You' and another song of theirs, 'Emergency', which explains why I have behaved the way I have over the past couple of weeks.
The songs are:
Joshua Kadison—'Beautiful in my Eyes'. Every word in this song describes my love for you.
ABC—'All of my Heart', which describes my hope for a future with you ... one more chance?

Bryan Adams—'Not Guilty', which kind of sums up the legal hassles we've had and my frustration at the law interfering with our problem, and my punishment not fitting the crime etc.
And our Roachford songs.
Libby, I want so much for you to call me—to see me—to love me again. If I make the mistake of 'hassling' you unintentionally, please forgive me.
Libby, I love you. I know that things can and will be different if you give me that one chance.

Phillip
xxxx

These were words she'd heard in part before and had braced herself against. But when he wrote like this, her heart and mind played tricks on her. She read the letter again and felt she could detect a man apologising for crimes yet committed. Somehow, she couldn't destroy the letters.

Libby arrived a little late for her dinner appointment. Shane had already arrived and was sitting in the Brazil Café, at a table facing North Steyne beach. The café owners had fastened back the concertina doors and a cool sea breeze wafted in through the Norfolk pines across the road.

'Libby!' Shane greeted her warmly.

'Ah, Shane,' Libby replied softly.

The pair embraced. Libby gratefully accepted his welcome and as soon as they sat down, poured her heart out. She needed someone who she felt safe with, who would listen without judging. Her mind was wracked with fear, her confidence dissolved. She wanted complete closure, some sense of protection from the coming avalanche. As she told Shane all that had happened, she gazed across the road toward the beach. Then her eyes fixed upon an eerie vision. Her pulse quickened. Her breaths shortened. Directly across from the cafe, she noticed someone standing behind one of the tall pine trees lining the beach. It seemed that the person was using the trunk of the tree as a hiding post from which to spy on her. She knew: it was Hopkins. She stopped her story mid-sentence.

'He's found me again,' she said quietly.

'What's wrong?' Shane asked, trying to see what Libby had spotted.

'Shane, it's him. He's just there.'

'Who, Hopkins?'

'He's done it again,' Libby said, cradling her forehead in her hands. Her shock had turned to emptiness. It was as if she'd lost another round in a fight she was never meant to win.

'What do you want me to do?' Shane asked, energised by Hopkins' presence.

Libby felt stronger by Shane's side and decided that she must seize this opportunity to ignore him. She had to get on with her life. The message was best delivered now. She would show him that he was no longer welcome in her life; there would be no friendship with him, no contact of any kind. He had broken all the rules—he had to understand his obsession must end. She was in another man's presence, not so vulnerable in public.

They carried on with their dinner as if he wasn't there. From ordering entrée through to finishing dessert an hour passed and Hopkins had not budged from his spot behind the pine tree. His patience astounded Shane. The man just glared from across the road, without flinching. He made an awkward table guest, contaminating their every bite.

'Shane, what I wanted to ask you,' Libby explained, 'was to be with me when I told this creep again that it was all over. His games have to stop. I can't do it on my own; I don't stand a chance without you here. The court case doesn't stop the way he feels. I know that.'

'I understand. I thought that was the case. He's clever too. He's about 90 metres away, far enough to argue his compliance with the AVO,' Shane said, now leaning over to hold the wrist of her right hand. 'You can't go through any more of this. I mean that. I'll do whatever it takes to help. Let him take on someone his own size for a change and stop lurking in the dark.' Libby was so relieved by Shane's words, she leaned over to hold his hand. It was a spontaneous reaction—and probably the worst thing she could have done in view of an unpredictable Phillip Hopkins.

In a millisecond, Hopkins was standing a metre away from their table, arms folded, face red with rage, veins swelling at his temple.

'What do you think you're bloody well doing?' Phillip bellowed. 'Who's it going to be, Libby, me or him?'

'Why don't you shut your mouth and leave her alone?' Shane said.

'This has nothing to do with you, buddy. Butt out.'

'Stop it,' Libby said. 'It's all over between us, totally, forever and if I have to have Shane here to make sure you don't hurt me, well, there you have it. You can't hurt me now, so please leave and never contact me again.'

Libby knew it was the soft option, rejecting him in another man's presence. But it was also the safer option.

Hopkins remained still for two seconds, before turning towards the beach, contemplating his next move. There was nothing he could do—outnumbered and outsmarted in unfamiliar circumstances, before an audience of the other cafe patrons, who had stopped eating to take in the confrontation.

Shane and Libby watched Hopkins until he was out of sight, some 200 metres down the road. They leaned back in their chairs, unnerved. 'Forget him, it's over,' Shane whispered.

Libby smiled and thanked him for his strength. She agreed that Hopkins was gone, but inside she knew he'd be back. She knew he wouldn't accept such an ignominious defeat. His challenge had just grown larger.

After coffee Shane paid the bill and they left, Shane walking Libby to her car. She thanked him again with a peck on the cheek and he offered to put her up at his place until the dust had settled. She assured him that she'd organised her own hiding place for the short term and, after all, she couldn't stay away from work and her own home for much longer.

Life had to resume eventually. She was now determined to begin the next phase.

'He can't change my life any longer, Shane. He can't do that, I won't let him.'

'You're right but you've got my number. Talk to the police about today and I'll make a statement about his breach of the AVO. Don't hesitate to call when you need to! I'm happy to testify.'

New Year was not a joyous time for Libby, but she was determined to start this year with some degree of vigour. She awoke at her sister's house in Manly. Her brother-in-law Mark suggested she come with him and his daughter to the Manly Swim Centre. She began the short walk up the hill to her parents' house at Balgowlah to grab her swimmers. As she passed the pool beyond her sister's house, she spotted Hopkins' red Laser in the car park. He was in the driver's seat. She was determined to continue with the day she had planned. As she quickened her pace, passing the car park, he manoeuvred the Laser in front of her, blocking her path. He jumped out of the car and approached her swiftly.

'Now that I've got you alone, I want you to tell me why you don't love me anymore.'

'I don't love you, stop hassling me,' she said calmly.

He grabbed her by the shoulders. At first she couldn't move, but eventually she managed to break from his grasp, dashing across four lanes of traffic, back the way she had come towards her sister's house. She stayed close to a young couple walking down the hill. Hopkins returned to his vehicle and Libby ran now to her sister's house and borrowed Mark's car to make the journey to her parents' house. As she pulled up outside, he was right behind, driving down the street only seconds after she'd opened the gate. He was like a blowfly drawn to sweat.

An hour later she walked into the swim centre with her brother-in-law and niece. For a while she thought she'd given him the slip, but he was there again to greet her. Mark spotted him too, but urged Libby to ignore him. Hopkins wasn't so patient with his surveillance this time round. Ten minutes later, he walked up to their spot on the grass.

'Go away, Phillip,' Mark said, as Hopkins stood over them, glaring at Libby.

'This is none of your business,' he replied.

'It is my business because I'm here with Libby and my daughter.'

'What are you going to do about it?'

'Would you like to see what I'm going to do about it?' Mark said standing up.

'Go ahead mate, I'll charge you with assault.'

Mark wasn't buying the bluff and promptly shoved Hopkins in the chest. Oddly, it was enough to force Hopkins to walk away. But he didn't go far and badgered the pair from several metres away. As Mark approached a lifeguard, Hopkins called, 'Come on mate, hit me right in the face.'

The lifeguard grabbed Hopkins and had staff call police immediately. Minutes later they arrived at the centre where a small crowd had gathered to watch the disturbance. As the officers approached the now corralled Hopkins, he jumped out of his chair.

'That's him,' he shouted, pointing to Mark. 'He's the one who assaulted me.'

Libby intervened. 'There is a court order, Constable, that says he can't come near me and he keeps following me. He should be locked up.'

'Is there an AVO on you mate?' One of the officers asked him.

'No,' he replied.

Before long Hopkins was being questioned in an interview room at Manly Police Station. 'There's an AVO out on you Phillip,' explained the officer who had been advised about the charges relating to Hopkins' assault on Libby when he dragged her along the footpath. He wanted Hopkins to confess to breaching his AVO.

'Did you assault Miss Masters?'

'Yes,' he replied. 'But we've since reconciled, we made up on Boxing Day. Ask her. We met and spent a few days together.'

In another interview room, Libby confirmed their meeting: 'I did meet with him,' Libby admitted. 'Not at his place, not at mine.' 'He said over and over again that he wouldn't leave me alone unless I saw him face to face. AVOs weren't keeping him away, the threat of court, police, none of that scares him. I had to try what I had left. We met, I asked him to leave me alone and he said what he had to say. That's it. I will do anything to stop this. You don't understand.'

Hopkins argued in the next room that this was clearly a breach engineered and agreed to by Libby. The police were stumped.

They could hardly charge Hopkins if Libby had somehow agreed to a meeting. There was a suggestion at the station that Libby would need to be charged as well, so neither process was an option.

Hopkins was released and warned to keep clear ... or else.

The confrontation at the pool and the subsequent interviews at the police station deflated Libby immensely—it was an exhausting end to an incredible year. All her attempts to eradicate him from her life had failed and she now faced the fact that his obsession was nowhere near at an end. Each day throughout 1996 would be a separate, draining battle.

PART THREE:
RELENTLESS

8

IN HER FACE

'Get up! Wake up! Wake up, you!'

Libby was startled awake. There was a hand rubbing her exposed shoulder. Her eyes shot open.

'What?' she screamed, jumping out of her bed. It was only her mother, standing over her bed. She was simply trying to get her daughter up and off to work. The room was drenched in sunlight. This was not another terrifying episode in the middle of the night. It was a bright morning in early February 1996. Her mother had spent the night with her in her old bed. There was no way she would have been able to get to sleep otherwise.

'Thank God', Libby sighed. 'Oh Mum, it's so good to see you, you don't know. I'm shaking.'

'It's almost 9 o'clock, Libby, you are so late,' warned her mother.

It didn't matter. Nights without sleep, without threat, were a rarity. She'd cherish this beautiful sunny morning, as if it was her last. Hopkins had obviously been busy elsewhere. He hadn't left his calling card the previous night and Libby was greatly relieved, but not stupid enough to think he'd left her alone for good.

A month had passed and Libby hadn't heard a word from police officer Rowan Haddock. Either Simone Crowe couldn't be found, or she wasn't keen on confronting the past. She didn't press Rowan for the information. There was so much going on and her few attempts to speak to him were met with grumpy replies from desk sergeants promising reluctantly to pass on messages. Rowan had been rostered on mid-dawn shifts in the patrol car and was hard to pin down.

Hopkins' midnight visits to her parents home at Balgowlah continued. Libby's mother empathised with what was happening to her daughter and even her father began to fathom what was going on late at night, even if he remained unconvinced of the regular harassment pattern. Hopkins continued throwing plastic balls on the roof and tapping at the window at all hours. And the assault case was set down for hearing. It was expedited because of Libby's reports of him breaching his AVO.

So Libby spent an afternoon in the witness box. Hopkins' solicitor questioned her aggressively, painting her as a psychopath who'd incited Hopkins into a tormented state of mind. The magistrate seemed compelled by what he'd heard from neighbours about Hopkins' nighttime visits. Despite pleading otherwise, Hopkins was found guilty. His lawyers asked for sentencing immediately; Libby knew that his family was nervous about the possibility of media coverage of the case, which would be damaging to his father's corporate reputation and would embarrass the family. Today there were no reporters present and the magistrate agreed to return after lunch with a decision.

Libby didn't stay for the sentencing, hearing the news by phone later. He'd been given a good behaviour bond, a lettuce leaf slap on the cheek. No conviction would be recorded if Hopkins stayed out of trouble for twelve months.

The prosecutor sighed, but he hadn't expected much more. Libby couldn't figure it out. He had brutally assaulted her. Without assistance from the neighbours, she might have been permanently injured. The superficial nature of her injuries had been highlighted again and again by Hopkins' side. Perhaps that swayed the outcome in his favour. She knew that no matter what, the assault charge wouldn't diminish his attitude and resolve. He would be enraged at being outed; at being embarrassed before his parents and family. Their knowledge of what had been going on might temporarily curtail his behaviour, but not for long. As she had discovered, Hopkins was a violent, obsessed stalker.

Libby never heard back from Haddock, but Libby discovered later that, like most of the officers who'd been called out to rescue Libby late at night, he followed her case closely.

Simone Crowe was a traumatised young woman, who had no desire to contact another victim, even a victim of a man she'd tried so hard to blank from her mind. Libby had done all she could to coax Simone out of her self-imposed anonymity—to no avail.

Meanwhile, Libby sank into depression and began to see a local psychiatrist. These were extremely emotional meetings, as she struggled with the reality of daily life and the fading hope of intervention from outside. On the nights he turned up, the local police night car would arrive and the familiar eye-rolling would ensue. They never found him, but as they left, officers could often hear her quiet sniffling at the door.

She would never return to Mosman. She moved in with her parents at Balgowlah full time and tried hard to resume a near-normal life, but she couldn't sleep. Every so often, just when she'd almost forgotten the name Phillip Hopkins, she'd sight him briefly, across the road from the cafe or restaurant she was visiting, late into the night. This she knew would have involved an all-night operation to tail her from work or home, monitoring her movements from bar to taxi to restaurant. Then he'd pause at the front window, or appear like a cat on the roof of the premises across the road from where she was dining. Libby fantasised about ways of catching him once and for all. She'd lie awake at night, deprived of sleep, imagining using steel traps to break his legs as he stalked the property. She took great pleasure in thinking of ways to torture him after he became trapped. Or perhaps she could recruit one of her male friends and together they could shoot him dead. That was the point she'd reached.

These fleeting daytime appearances were different from his nighttime visits, which were still part of his weekly routine. Whereas a voice or a tap at the window in the darkness would terrify her, his daily pursuit was the slow-cooked version. The repetitive and mentally nauseating process of wearing Libby down, keeping her on edge, nervous and ill at ease. She'd jump at the sound of car horns, or any sudden noise around her. Libby didn't know which was worse—but she did know that until she could prove what was happening, this was her life. She detested every living hour, unable to see an end to the psychological persecution.

Libby returned to the company of her friends, in particular Sarah and Shane, spending a little more time out with them, rather than rugged up at home with her parents, peering constantly at the back fence. Life had to go on and she was curious to see how courageous Phillip was with an audience, if he dared breach the current AVO and whether her socialising would bring an end to his night visits—if only.

On the third Saturday in February, Libby, Sarah and another friend, Patrick, decided to dare fate and hit the Oaks. It was time to wipe the slate clean. The girls were loud together, gregarious, just like the old days, when they went out to see what was on offer. A few hours into the night, Hopkins turned up, at the other end of the main bar. Libby spotted him first; she was too fragile not to be scouring the room. He sent her stares and evil looks from across the room. Sarah suggested they call the police. He was, after all, within the 100-metre limit of his AVO. Sarah wondered whether he had come there to hassle Libby deliberately or if he'd been coming to the Oaks regularly.

Just as Libby had relaxed enough to become ensconced in conversation with her friends, Hopkins walked by within arm's length.

'Christ, you're ugly!' he said as he drew level.

Sarah was about to have her say, until Libby grabbed her by the arm. She didn't want to have anything else slapped in her face. Hopkins continued however. 'You're a hooked-nose Jew. Look at you,' he snarled.

When Hopkins left the bar, Libby asked both women to remember what had happened, just in case she needed their help.

Three weeks later, at a nightclub in Cremorne, Libby was out again with her friends, including Shane. At about 11pm, Hopkins showed up, seemingly intoxicated and ready to get in Libby's face. He began by following the group of friends around the nightclub, from the main bar and dance-floor to the piano bar upstairs.

He kept his distance and this time the group was not giving him any benefit of the doubt—he was there to cause trouble. He thrust his middle finger up at her so pointedly it caught the attention of others in the club. He couldn't resist a verbal shot either, 'Just slutting around again are you, Libby?' he said, from several metres away.

Again Libby had to stop her friends, particularly Shane, from launching a return attack. She wanted there to be no ambiguity for Hopkins to use against her. He would be the only aggressor. Then an hour later, as the group returned to the bar to purchase another round of drinks, Hopkins approached quickly. 'I loved you; you know I loved you.' He pointed at her.

She said nothing. Shane jostled him and they glared at each other, before Hopkins did a U-turn and walked out. This time, Libby notified the police and they took statements from the group.

The following weekend, however, before the police acted, Libby found herself confronted once more, across the harbour at the Basement, a popular jazz venue. Hopkins was inside the women's toilets. As she emerged from her cubicle, there he was, away from his haunts, never letting go of his target.

The shock of his presence, not just at the Basement, but inside the women's toilets, infuriated Libby. She headed straight for the bouncers at the entrance and asked the club to make contact with the nearest police station. She had been pushed too far and she wanted action, now.

The bouncers rounded him up and, soon after, the police turned up to take him back to The Rocks police station. The officers contacted the police on the north side who were handling Libby's most recent allegations.

Hopkins claimed that he was at the Basement to see that night's acts, that Libby was a freak. Then he suddenly calmed down and asked to use the conveniences. Officers showed Hopkins out of the interview room and he headed to the men's room, across the open workroom of the station. Hopkins saw the huge, unmanned front desk facing George Street, took a sharp right and jumped across it, before regaining his feet and escaping through the double front doors.

At just past midnight Hopkins ran west up Argyle Street, watched by rowdy onlookers outside the bustling Orient Hotel opposite. What seemed like a whole station full of police surged out of two exits on foot and gave chase. Within ten seconds, three officers had tackled Hopkins 50 metres up the hill, on the hard, old convict-lain cobble stones, as he tried to evade apprehension by running towards the road.

He was charged with escaping lawful custody and breaching an existing AVO, and transported to Sydney Police Station for a late-night bail sergeant to decide his immediate fate. It was not only the justice system that Hopkins had to worry about now; a frantic police chase up Argyle Street could not avoid media notice and the stalker was about to have his deeds spread to a much wider audience.

The article in the next morning's *Sun Herald* briefly outlined Hopkins' thwarted escape and his breach of his AVO. It was only a short story, but it was enough to trigger two astonishing events.

Soon after his attempted escape, Libby received a chilling nighttime phone call from a most unexpected source.

'It's Malcolm, Libby, Malcolm Hopkins.'

'Yes, what do you want, Mr Hopkins?' She was stunned.

He started by saying he'd always hoped that Libby would be the one capable of turning her son around. He needed saving, needed to settle down.

Libby attempted to underline his son's problems in the kindest way possible. 'There is something mentally wrong with your son Mr Hopkins—there has to be for him to act the way he does. He must be stopped; he's cruel,' she said calmly.

There was silence for a moment. 'I'm sorry if he's been troubling you and you have every right not to be in this relationship, but can I give you my wife's phone number. Maybe you'd like to have a woman to woman talk. He's a good boy really, Libby. He doesn't mean any harm, I promise.'

Libby wasn't arguing anymore. She agreed to think about what Malcolm had said and quickly terminated the call. That such an astute businessman would have thought that these traumatic events could be washed away by a phone call between two women astounded her.

Phillip Hopkins' dramatic arrest at The Rocks hadn't only spurred his father into action, it had caught the eye of at least one crucial former player in his tawdry life.

9

NOT ALONE

When the phone rang on her desk at work, Libby sensed that there was something strange about the call. She didn't know what or why, but she hesitated for one drawn-out second. She quickly dismissed her paranoia and told herself it was a work call. But it was not.

It was yet another surprise caller.

'Um, is that Libby Masters? It's Simone Crowe calling.'

'Who? Oh, Simone Crowe. That Simone Crowe ... I mean, Phillip's ex. I know you, yes, hello ... ', said Libby stammering in surprise and excitement.

'I read about his escape and I felt I had to call.'

'Thanks for calling. You know all about Phillip Hopkins, right?'

'Know about him? Oh yeah ... he stalked me for eight whole years. He bashed me. He changed me forever ... I know him alright and I wish to God I'd never ever met him.

'I saw the story and thought long and hard about it and had to do something, before ... ' she tailed off. 'I don't know why I'm doing this, but I couldn't believe that ten years later, he was still driving women nuts. Maybe my conscience got the better of me. I don't know.'

'That's fine, I'm glad it did.' Libby slowly leaned back on her chair and pulled the phone closer carefully to avoiding disconnecting the call or missing a single word. This was the call she'd been waiting for. Her life was echoing this woman's; she needed to share that synchronicity.

She was about to ask Simone a question, when the other woman's story began: 'I met him at a club. He came up and reckoned he'd seen me before somewhere. I've thought about that moment eight million times.

He wasn't the exciting type. Not boring either, just normal, I thought. I was only twenty. I didn't think he was bad looking. He wasn't pushy and I was curious as to where he'd seen me before. He kept that little secret for a long time. None of that twigged. It was a con to crack onto me.

'The day after I'd first heard about you, Libby, I thought I saw him in the street. It's such a horrible feeling to see someone you think looks like him. He was my hunter and I was his prey. It makes me so sick to even think about it ... '

Simone paused. Libby sensed her tears. 'Go on, take your time,' she coaxed.

'I think he expected sex the first night we met, you know. I wouldn't, I couldn't. I don't do that so soon. We did though, a couple of weeks later, because he became pushy and was offended by my refusals. I was just not sure who he was ... I haven't thought about that for so long. Is it any wonder?

Over the next few months, I slowly got used to him, got into it, got into him, but he became so moody when he didn't get his way. That was my first experience of his sick mind. It didn't bother me enough. That was the problem. We got more entrenched, more like a couple. When he got into one of those moods, he was pretty bloody awful, not just to me—my friends hated him. He made such a fool of himself in public, pleading with me to keep away from my friends, it was embarrassing ... and then he'd be like a complete baby afterwards. He'd say sorry and ... '

'Say how he had a crap upbringing, a dysfunctional family?' Libby interjected.

'Absolutely, that's exactly what he'd say.'

'And you felt sorry for him again.' Libby smiled.

'I did. You did too?'

'Yep, like a fish on the end of a hook.'

'I thought I was the dumbest sucker in Australia,' Simone said. 'You too, hey? He even told me he once punched his mother. He knocked her down in the kitchen. His attitude to her, to his family, was just shit. For his 21st birthday his parents gave him this really nice stereo. I was there and I thought it was wonderful and yet he hated it. It wasn't good enough.

It wasn't big enough. It wasn't expensive enough. And it wasn't the one he'd told his dad to buy. So ungrateful.'

'I didn't see too many friends in his life either … maybe that should have made me twig,' Libby added.

'Yeah, no friends, not even from work. When we were together, he was sacked from his job. He smashed his boss and was given his marching orders. He had every excuse under the sun about why he had to do it. The only friend I ever saw him hang around with was Jason—an oaf. Yeah, they were as thick as thieves, Jason and … ' Simone paused. 'I almost said his name, but I can't without feeling ill. I haven't said it for years. Anyway, his mate would always stick up for him, like some salivating lap dog.'

'After six months together, it all went mad. I tried so hard to end it. And when I thought I had, I hadn't. I can't explain it.'

'I think I know what you mean … he pretends that it's not over and jokes about your state of mind. As if I didn't mean to end it,' Libby said, shaking her head.

'Even after the violence, he claimed I'd never break it off, that I couldn't live on without him.'

'How violent did it get?' Libby asked.

Simone paused again, sighed and continued with her story. 'I can't go through the full detail of it all, Libby. I just can't. I'm sorry, but some things you need to know. In my flat sometimes, when I wouldn't have sex with him, he'd drag me into this room, half joking initially, and half serious. He'd lock me in there. It was an empty study room. No furniture, nothing. I had to sit on the cold wooden floor. There were bars on all the windows. He tied the door to. If I tried to force it or break out, he'd come in and whack me, in this frantic half-joking way. He'd throw me against the wall, Libby. I'd be in mid-air and my back would smash against the wall. He even locked me in his mother's room one time. I couldn't get out. I was stuck there, even after they got home. He waited until his own mother walked upstairs and found me there. I had to explain. Make up some bullshit about a migraine. It was gross, it was so sick. He loved it. Then we'd go through the remorseful stage straight afterwards … and I bought it. I bought it for almost nine months.'

'Did he go off in one of those rages, if he got jealous?' Libby asked.

'Sure did. He'd destroy all my TAFE drawings, all my art. He'd tear it to pieces like some mad, uncaring dog. That was before my art went dark ... before I turned inside out and kept away from everyone, anyone ... I just felt dirty, violated, guilty. Even the cakes I baked at home with the rest of my flatmates weren't safe ... when he felt like it, he'd just lose it, lose it completely and throw the cakes all over the place ... It would take us ages to clean up. That was when I was lucky. He was soon constantly punching, shoving and hitting me. He'd knock me on the ground over virtually nothing, kick me in the stomach, in the back, in the back of the head—all the places that wouldn't show. Occasionally he'd strike my face.

He had this flat above a shop in Concord and he once dragged me from the top floor, from his bedroom, after punching me in the face. I was covered in blood. He dragged me by the hair down two flights of stairs! He kicked me and hurt me in all the places it wouldn't show. He was too gutless to be caught. By the way, did he hurt you?'

Libby was taken aback at first. 'Yeah, he forced himself upon me a few times and I gave in, just to avoid the drama, of him "accidentally" hitting me. So, did he stalk you when the relationship ended?'

Simone laughed, a clinical, false laugh. 'He stalked me alright—endlessly. I ran away, to Tamworth, to Mum's place. I had no choice. He broke into my house, punched me in the face and gave me two black eyes. He'd wake me up at 3am, sitting on top of the shed out the back.

He followed me to the club, to restaurants, to bars. He'd scream at me in a room full of diners and slam the door in disgust. He'd park around the corner and wait for me for hours over the weekend, then just drive away. Even at my father's place, he'd throw something at the window, I'd wake up and he'd be sitting in the long grass at the back, peering out so that his eyes were shiny in the moonlight.

I was petrified every single night. I'd vomit. I got so sick. I had to take time off work. He'd be sitting in the back of my bus of an afternoon. He must have taken other buses other days and missed me so often. But he was mad enough to play this game of hide and seek for so long.'

Simone explained how she had taken out AVOs. How police involvement proved fruitless. Hopkins just got smarter, more elusive, better at stalking. 'I tried to run away too, twice.'

'Where to?' Libby asked.

'I went to the country, as I said, to my mother in Tamworth. I even started a new life ... enrolling in an arts course. He found me, travelled all the way up there and stalked me again. In fact I think he enjoyed Tamworth best. He lived in this hire car, from what I could tell, and roamed the streets and backyards at night. He got brazen there. He confronted me, Mum, my TAFE teachers and threatened to kill me. He threatened to kill anyone who got in the way, even Mum. He stole a photo album from my car that I'd brought up to show my mother. A week later, some of the photos of us together were glued to the bonnet of my car, with droplets of blood stuck to them. It was creepy. The local cops didn't know what to do. They treated it all as a bad domestic and told us to go back to Sydney and sort it out. That's when I decided to leave. I had to leave the whole goddamn country. I went overseas. It was the only real choice I had left—or kill him!'

'You went overseas because of him?'

'You bet. I was on the verge of killing myself, or killing him. Forget what he was threatening to do to me. I had to go and it worked. For two and a half years, I was free of him. I lived in England. I had a kind of boyfriend over there. I got my life back. I was rid of him, although I lost my friends, my family and the place I grew up in. I loved Sydney so much before I met him. I loved so many things before I met him. The beaches were once beautiful. The city was incredible once upon a time. The smell of the place, the sights, they've since soured. I use to love me too, but it's just too complicated now.'

Even 17,000 kilometres away, Simone had constant nightmares. Her recurring dream involved being stabbed by Hopkins, stabbed in the stomach. It never went away. Eventually, she came home, back to her family and friends. She had to in the end, and simply hope that Hopkins had moved on, had perhaps even married and grown out of his cruel behaviour.

'So you had to go overseas to make the break? Is that what I have to do?'

'It won't work, Libby. Within weeks of finding a place, registering my telephone and gas, he found me at Alexandria!'

'He found you after two and a half years?'

'Yep, as if I hadn't been away for a single day. As soon as I was in Sydney again, he was onto me. How he knew that I'd returned is still a mystery to me. Unless all that geeky computer work he does has him tapped into some public utility mainframe. I wouldn't be surprised. I had flatmates, which was probably the best insurance policy I could have had. They saw most of the next round of stalking, the cruel obsession and his nastiness. They saved my life and sanity. But yes, the stalking was back on again ... the persistent hunter, over my shoulder, across the road, in the bushes, against the window, above the shop and even in the shopping centre toilets. He was bloody untiring. I became a wreck all over again.' Simone was clearly exhausted by revisiting her nightmare.

'He stooped even lower though, Libby. He went through my garbage bin, again and again. He broke into our flat and stole stuff ... God knows what. But what spooked me most was the night I finished work at the pub. I walked to the car park and he'd spread more photos from my album over my car, the album he stole in Tamworth years before ... and again, covered them in blood spots. They were glued to my car bonnet. It was so sick, just so upsetting. I didn't know where he was at that moment, whether he was behind another car in the dark, or even inside my own. I cried for days.'

Neither woman spoke for a long time. They couldn't, until Simone said what Libby was waiting so desperately to hear.

'But it did end, Libby. It just took time.'

'What do you mean? Do you mean you've got to be prepared to go the full eight years with him?'

'Yes and no,' said Simone, who sounded suddenly buoyant. 'Yes, eight years must have got to him too. It must have bored him. Plus, I was surrounded by people in the end. I had to be. He freaked me out so much. My flatmates psyched him out a little bit I reckon. They dogged him and somehow hurled as much back as he gave. He continually embarrassed himself. I kept his mother updated on his behaviour too. That was the killer. That really nailed him.'

'You spoke to Kathryn Hopkins about his stalking?'

'Sure did. She didn't believe me at first. She wouldn't talk to me. But I used some of his techniques—I harangued her. I forced her to take my calls and listen. And although she never accepted what he was doing, I think she helped end it. I'm sure she did.'

'But Phillip treats his mother like his father does. How could she change his ways?'

'I don't know. But I told her about the bashings and the doctor's reports I had. I had a few recordings of his telephone conversations too. This didn't ever scare him, but his parents couldn't contemplate their son being outed publicly. Their status in the community, his father's status in the corporate world, could never be compromised. That's all they have. They don't have much of a family.'

By now Simone was positively on fire, sounding almost victorious. It all made sense, thought Libby: the threats to his family, the reverse stalking by Simone's flatmates and her determination never to be alone. The predator's fun had been taken away from him. How could she possibly replicate that though? The recent court appearances were done and dusted. Virtually nothing was made public, the Hopkins family made sure of it. She had nothing really to hold over them.

Libby knew she was in no position to start shacking up with a bunch of local uni students, whose lives and hours were so different to that of her own. The same plan was untenable for her, but the answer to Libby's predicament was here somewhere, it had to be. Both women were exhausted.

'You know where, how and almost always when he stalks, right?' Simone asked finally.

'Well, yeah.'

'I thought about this many years later, but wasn't smart enough to do it at the time. Forget the coppers, why not stalk him yourself?'

'What me, I can't—'

'No, why can't you employ someone to stalk him? Why can't you get people to follow him, to take pictures of him?'

'I don't know, I guess I can.'

'Find a real private investigator who can prove to the courts that he's breaching his AVO and his bond. You've waited for the police to move, but you've never had any real proof that paints the whole picture, the frequency. Set a trap. Set him up. Stalk him yourself! But you'll have to count me out,' Simone added. 'I've been recovering from eight years of this shit. Never again. Those all-night vigils almost killed me. I want to help, Libby, but it's up to you now. If he comes back into my life somehow, I won't be able to cope. I'll top myself.'

Libby couldn't argue with any of that. Simone's techniques and advice had given her enormous strength, but there was clearly a limit to what one person, one victim could bear. Enough was enough. They ended the call warmly, wishing each other the best. Libby knew she probably wouldn't hear from Simone again. The call had been a small window back to the past; Simone had no intention of jumping through. But now Libby's mind was brimming with ways of doing what Simone had suggested, of stalking the stalker.

That night, Libby paced the house, ideas buzzing around in her head. It was nearing 8pm and close to sunset. Her parents had left for the week on a trip out of town they'd been planning and looking forward to for sometime. Being on her own was a real test of her resolve. Nights out with her friends were easier to get through, even allowing for the chance Hopkins might turn up, but being home alone was never a time to cherish. Motivated, however, by Simone's call, Libby had gone down to Manly straight after work to do a bit of shopping and was planning to cook up a tasty meal.

Before her parents had left, her father had spoken about employing a lighting contractor to attach a few additional sensor lights to the rear of the house. While Libby didn't think for a second that the lights would ward off her deranged stalker, the sole sensor they had didn't do much good. Perhaps a few more might put him off his routine. What would be the point of stalking at night when night turned to day as he entered the yard? But the installation was yet to be booked, so for now it would remain dark out there, whether he showed up or not.

As night fell Libby stood up from the couch and locked the sliding doors. She returned to the kitchen to wash up and as she ran the hot water, she looked up at the hall clock. It was ten-thirty and a strong wind had blown up. She wanted to clear up and then get as much sleep as possible. Libby could never tell whether it was going to be one of those nights. And on blustery nights like this one, every sound, all the thuds, creaks and clangs, were construed as one thing: Hopkins in the dark yard outside.

As she turned the hot water tap off, she was startled by an almighty crash outside the the bathroom. She realised she'd left the single bathroom window open and ran out of the kitchen down the corridor. She held her breath, listening. It had to be him. Had he fallen, trying to get inside? As she slowed down at the end of the hallway to turn the corner into the open space in front of the bathroom, she could hear a scratching noise directly outside. She grabbed an umbrella from the stand and approached slowly.

'Time to scare me again, is it Phillip? You are so gutless.'

There was no reply. She walked into the bathroom and slammed the open window shut, before bolting it closed. Libby leaned against the sink and wondered for one frightening second whether she was really alone in the house. Had Hopkins actually got in? Was the noise she heard not a fall on the outside, but him falling into the house?

'I'm calling the police!' Libby said loudly.

As soon as she said it, she heard a noise under the house. She froze, listening for the sound. She shuffled slowly down the hallway, past all the darkened bedrooms, on her way to the telephone. Her footsteps seemed loud, as intimidating as whatever was under the house. She made it into the lounge room, eyes darting from left to right. She picked up the receiver and the dial tone pierced the pulsating silence. She quickly rang triple-0, but then as the operator's voice asked her for details, she just stood there, frozen by the redundancy of what she was about to do. She listened to the voice on the other end requesting a reply and simply hung up, resigned to another night of tension. Libby realised that the noises may not have been Phillip Hopkins, but that was the power of his torment. His potential appearance was enough.

At three-thirty she was still awake, curled up on her couch, monitoring every sound, every branch brushing against the wall in the wind. She kept a knife close by. She didn't care whether she'd have to use it or not. His life was of no significance to her now. As the late, late movie flickered too brightly for her heavy, sore and red eyes, she realised she'd been gutted by her own paranoia. The pre-dawn silence was broken by the sound of a small dog barking from the adjoining property. She wondered whether the dog knew when Hopkins entered the area and wondered whether she herself needed a dog.

She sniggered quietly. Like that would make a difference. Libby stood up, proceeded to walk into her bedroom, still giggling in a self-mocking fashion. She passed by one of the hallway mirrors and stopped. She saw a haggard young girl with stress wrinkles under her bloodshot eyes and a face that went from laughing to crying almost instantly.

Then a flash of light reflected in the mirror. She turned and looked through the locked sliding doors. The light appeared again. It was him, under the frangipani, next to the back shed. Moments later, the light and the intruder were gone. She tried to follow the trail with her eyes, standing on tiptoes to see over the back fence, but it was no good. The trail of torchlight snaked its way back through the bushes on the property at the rear and a body hurled itself over the adjoining fence. He'd left it late, but now he was done for the night. The simple fact that she had seen him fulfilled his twisted mission.

10

INTERFERENCE

Rob Hearn was a self-employed private investigator based in Neutral Bay. He worked for himself and by himself on most cases. He was young—27—and keen to impress. His fees were modest, as he was still building a client base. Libby was prepared to pay whatever it took. They met at a time when Libby thought Hopkins would not be watching, early one weekday morning.

Rob looked more like a tradesman than a private investigator and Libby liked him straightaway. He was serious about his work. He was not in it to work on women. And he was instantly enthusiastic about the job at hand. He discussed with her the fact that Hopkins would have what he called a 'launching point'.

'He comes from over the back fence,' she told him, 'and from what I've seen, heads west afterwards for quite a few backyards, but I don't know where he launches from. Why is that important?'

'He'll be launching under streetlights, where others can see him; where I might be able to see him and photograph him. If I don't know where it all starts from, it makes it difficult to track him. But we'll try.'

Libby went over the events again. Rob had to know what he was dealing with—how smart her ex was. By the sound of his modus operandi, Rob thought that Hopkins might be working from a textbook, a standard private investigation text like the ones Rob had used for his own training.

She twigged immediately and remembered once seeing a manual with a magnifying glass on the cover in Hopkins' flat.

For an entire month, Rob attempted to follow Hopkins from three locations: from work, his home and Libby's parents' backyard, on the seven occasions that she knew he was there. It was a full-time job and one that stretched Rob's patience and skill. Hopkins was quite adept at losing anyone he suspected of tailing his vehicle. Rob concluded that Hopkins had an array of different cars and spent nights at his office. At his home Hopkins was extra vigilant about who might be in the vicinity.

Early on Rob felt he'd been 'made' by Hopkins, which led to a different, more conservative stalking pattern. Only a stalker had the mental tools to beat another stalker. Each time Rob ventured into an adjoining yard to head Hopkins off during one of his nighttime adventures, Hopkins kept his distance, or Rob himself was outed by the family pets or other neighbours. On the two nights that Hopkins was actually heard to enter Libby's backyard, Rob had not been on duty. He had other clients to attend to and the wily stalker was able to detect that the coast was clear. It was like rubbing salt into a fresh wound and, for a while, he'd made Rob even angrier than Libby.

On one of the nights that Rob was not scheduled to keep guard on Libby, when her parents were out late at a function, Hopkins circled the house madly, hitting the walls at random, creeping about beneath the house and, to Libby's horror, bashing against the floorboards. It was the most frustrating time for Libby and an embarrassing period for the young PI, who'd promised so much and delivered so little. Hopkins was smarter than his pursuer had predicted, and even seemed to be enjoying the counter-stalking game. Rob felt his target was revelling in it.

Soon after evading Libby's newly appointed protector though, Hopkins made a crucial error in judgement. On a night that Libby had sensed Hopkins' presence, she tried calling Rob Hearn's mobile. She couldn't achieve a dial tone on her first go. That's odd, she thought, and tried again. On the second attempt she got through, and Rob said he was just knocking off at a job nearby and would be there in five minutes.

He pulled up some 100 metres from Libby's parents' house and quietly made his way down the darkened street and into the front yard. Seconds after knocking gently at the door, so as not to disturb whatever was happening out the back, he heard a car roar down the street towards him and turned. At that moment, Libby opened the door.

'Forget it; he went the moment I called you.'

Rob kept his eyes focused on the approaching car. It was Hopkins in his red Laser, slowing to a crawl outside the home. He wound down the passenger's side window facing the startled pair; he had no balaclava on.

'Everything okay then?' Hopkins yelled, before driving off at speed in the opposite direction.

When Libby looked at Rob, she saw that he had a smile stretching from ear to ear. Hopkins had forgotten the crucial ruling from the court that had handed down his bond. He was to keep 100 metres from Libby's house or he'd face the court again. 'We've got him. He's made a mistake. He can't be here, yet we have two people who can say he was.'

'Yes, that's right!'

Suddenly, after a period of exasperation and no apparent end to the stalking, Libby felt meek no more. Her hunch, to risk bringing in a stranger, had worked. Things moved swiftly. The police were brought in, statements made and a court case quickly arranged. Hopkins was charged again under new stalking legislation. Libby discovered that the new laws were created as a result of another case of persistent stalking that led to the murder of a young woman at the hands of her former partner. It was sobering news.

The elderly magistrate on duty at North Sydney Court was clearly not thrilled about having to deal with what he viewed as a domestic dispute. He appeared cynical of the new legislation, drawn up by politicians in haste and as a result of media pressure after a serious crime. He brushed aside the arguments of both the inexperienced police prosecutor and Hopkins' solicitor right from the start. He wanted to know who saw what and what was said. The allegation that Hopkins had said 'Everything okay then?' seemed to stick in his mind. He was curious about it, as if it was the key to any breach of Hopkins' orders.

'Why did your client say that?' the now fully engaged magistrate asked Hopkins' lawyer.

'Well, Your Honour, that brings us to the reason why this case against my client should be dispensed with immediately. I can prove to the court that Ms Masters was in an obvious state of distress on the night in question and on nights either side of the evening in question. Whether there was some dispute between her and Mr Hearn, who, you may have read, Your Honour, had been spending quite a deal of time harassing my client ... But whether there was a dispute there or not, Mr Hopkins didn't know. What he did know, however, was that given Ms Masters' history of phoning police, alleging all kinds of dastardly things, he was quite concerned for his former partner and was merely ensuring that she was okay.'

'Objection, Your Honour,' piped up the police prosecutor. 'Ms Masters was in no distress caused by investigator Rob Hearn. Where's the defence's evidence for this? It's pure speculation.'

'Objection overruled. Sit down, Sergeant,' demanded the magistrate.

'Well thank you, Your Honour,' the solicitor continued, snapping at his lapels and looking down at Libby's table. 'My client, sitting here beside me, had every reason to be concerned for Ms Masters. We know that they had a strong and faithful relationship despite their troubles documented in this very court a month ago. And we know Ms Masters has a predilection for emotional and tearful outbursts under stress. We present previous police reports to verify that. But it was what Ms Masters was doing that night which led my client to check on her. Can I please produce these phone records to the court, which belong to my client? All pages are part of the attached warrant. They clearly underline Ms Masters' confused and distressed state. These are phone records, traces on my client's line, Your Honour, which prove her infatuation with Phillip Hopkins.'

Libby couldn't keep quiet at this. 'Infatuated! You're kidding. He's infatuated with me. He's got the sick mind. When will anyone understand this?'

The magistrate's concentration was broken. 'One more outburst, Ms Masters, and you can get out of my courtroom and into a cell downstairs,' he said firmly. 'You are also asking the court to outlaw the defendant from attending places he has previously been known to attend, just because you turn up there too. I have some sizeable decisions to make and you're not helping.'

'You see, Your Honour, this is what she's capable of,' interjected Hopkins' solicitor.

'Hold on, let me have a look at these phone records.'

The magistrate read them twice. He blinked and dropped the papers on the oak bench in front of him, then removed his glasses.

'Sergeant, please step forward and sight these records. I'll then hear your submission and make my judgement on this alleged breach,' said the magistrate, before leaning back into his high arched seat.

Upon viewing the documents, the prosecutor returned to the table ashen-faced. He leaned over to Libby and whispered in her ear. 'What the hell were you doing calling his home 21 times that week?'

She didn't move a muscle. She was gobsmacked. What happened? she thought. Did I make those calls? No, I didn't. But why are they saying that?

'Who said I did?' Libby replied in a strained voice.

'Telstra records, traces made on calls received at his house, show that you phoned Phillip ten times that night. What do I say to the *beak* [judge] now, do you think?'

Libby leaned back in her seat. What really happened that night? She shook her head to acknowledge she had no answer, no explanation for the court. Hopkins was on the far side of the court, but managed to lean forward and catch her sickened gaze. He was smirking broadly. After she glimpsed his expression, she turned back quickly to the magistrate as if to plead for some explanation. There was none.

The rest of the short proceedings were a blur. Hopkins had been pestered by his alleged victim and he had indisputable proof. The magistrate found in his favour. He was prepared to continue the AVO orders but the breach allegations were dismissed. Now even Libby's closest friends and family had reason to doubt her. How did this happen? What could she ever do to fight back? She was annihilated. She was escorted from the court, bewildered.

As she shuffled out of the courtroom, heels dragging as she went, head bowed in defeat, a police officer blocked her way. 'You got a second?'

She looked up. It was the officer from Mosman who had collated her statements and evidence in the breach of AVO case against Hopkins. 'Sure.'

'Let that be a lesson to you, young girl. This is not a place to be toyed with. This is a court of law and while you go to these extreme lengths to hurt this bloke, you take me away from more serious cases—cases that involve life and death. Do you understand that?'

Libby had nothing left. She had no defence, no explanation, nothing. 'I'm sorry, but something else has happened here.'

'We don't want to hear it after that,' the sergeant said. 'You're lucky we don't charge you with public mischief. That could see you in jail, Miss. Now go home, get over him and don't ever call me again. Do you hear?'

'Yes,' Libby muttered.

As she walked from the court, out into the glaring sun, she stopped behind her mother for a second and turned to see Hopkins smiling, locked in an embrace with his mother on the court steps.

Libby turned away, staring into nothing and mumbled quietly to herself: 'I have to kill the bastard. I have to kill him now.'

Confused, ashamed and still fuming at the unexpected turn of events, Libby decided to burn off her frustration with a swim and then relax in the safety of the warm summer sun …

There was no safer sight than the little park under Anthony's tiny Melbourne balcony. With winter just turning into spring, barren patches of earth were dotted with small tufts of green growth. The frost had passed and warmer weather was just around the corner. The park was a safe place, so far away from trouble, so foreign to the sick world she'd been living in. Tall pencil pines stood resolute in the cold wind. Their strength was reassuring. Dogs were scampering between the legs of their owners and tying themselves in knots with their leads. All her fears left her body on that balcony. If only she could stay here forever. But that could never work.

Anthony's smoky odour filled his apartment. This time, he was going nowhere. His weekend was dedicated to her. He could see she'd been to hell and back. He'd be there for her now, he told her. He would save her life, even if it endangered his own. Someone had to end her horrible torment; and it might as well be him. She was overwhelmed and buoyed by his commitment.

They sat together at the small dining room table and decided that there was no turning back, they would lure Hopkins to Melbourne, using a message sent to him, via Sarah, saying that Libby was tired of running. She wanted a new start, in a new state.

In Melbourne Hopkins' AVO no longer applied. This was neutral territory and the place where Hopkins would die.

The pistol Anthony bought from a gun dealer was shiny and menacing. She'd never seen anything like it before. It was real, loaded and waiting to end her nightmare.

She couldn't wait to meet Hopkins on St Kilda Pier late that afternoon as planned. As the light faded, his life would be taken with one pull of the trigger. Anthony would stalk the very best of stalkers.

They discussed the plan in the little flat and Anthony's fingers held the gun with ease—no hint of a shudder or nervous twitch. He was calm, empowered by its reassuring weight. There was just one hour to go; one hour to end it all, and Libby would be free. They could begin a new life together. Even if they were caught, life would eventually return to normal. They were prepared to take their chances with the law.

No one was going to change their minds. Libby was no longer the Libby she knew. Calmly planning her revenge brought a high she'd never experienced before. They held hands across the table, the gun between them. It was what had to be done. No one else was capable of ending this.

The tram trip down St Kilda Road seemed to last just a few seconds. She was deep in thought, focusing on how his face would look when he felt the barrel at his chest, saw Anthony's fingers squeezing the trigger. He would die from shock, she thought. He'd never imagine that she had the guts to recruit someone to kill him in cold blood. He deserved nothing but death. He would never return to haunt her again.

They stepped off the tram and onto the footpath.

They turned to each other and managed a smile. They held hands and hugged, Libby whispering, 'It's alright, it'll be alright. I can't live with him in the world any longer. I won't ... Thank you. I love you for this.'

They kissed and he turned back towards the city to get into his position. She watched him leave and she headed towards the beach. She walked off to meet Phillip for the very last time. She could see the beginning of the pier. Each step felt extremely light, not requiring effort or strain. She was ready.

Anthony doubled back around the main cluster of shops to keep out of the way of Hopkins' approach. The barrel of the pistol sat warmly in his overcoat pocket, as his hand gripped the handle tightly. He wasn't letting go.

An icy cold gust of wind hit Libby in the face. The sun was all but gone, the temperature close to freezing. Her heart pounded with excitement. Her eyes darted from side to side, then along the pier, trying to find the shape of the man she despised. She saw nothing except a long stretch of wooden boards leading out over the freezing water. Anthony had been right, no one was there at that time of the afternoon. The kiosk was closed and the fishermen gone. It was too late—and too early—for company.

As she stepped onto the first board, her low heels clapped on the wood and continued the beat as she took another step, then another and another. He may have been huddled in the shadows of the kiosk at the end of the pier, but she could not see from where she was. If Hopkins was there, he was exactly where they wanted him to be, in a dead end, with no way out.

All of a sudden something sprung out from the side of the pier, directly at Libby's head. She ducked and, as she regained her balance, she saw that it was a seagull she'd interrupted from a feed of rotting bait.

Then she heard a footstep on the boards somewhere behind her. She couldn't determine how far away with the wind whistling past her ears. She dared not stop to turn for fear of scaring him. He must be lured all the way. He always had an escape route, a back up plan—but not this time. Phillip was so far away from his playground that his guard would be down. That was why it had to happen here.

Libby's steps continued. The further she ventured out into the wind, the harder it was to hear the sound of his approach. She knew he was there though. He wouldn't be able to resist. She was only a few metres away from the kiosk and the noise of the steps behind was growing louder. Was he coming closer? She couldn't turn, but picked up her pace to take refuge under the kiosk's awning.

Just as she reached the closed kiosk, she reeled back as a man in a balaclava emerged from the other side of the building, tapping his shoes on the board. So, that was what she'd heard. This was as close as Phillip Hopkins had come to her in many months.

He knew he'd scared her almost to death and began snorting with laughter. She stood still, knowing that Anthony would be close, ready to end it all. Her heart pounded against her chest. Hopkins slowly removed his mask and softened his gaze.

'Sorry to frighten you, it's been a while,' he said calmly. 'You know me.'

Libby didn't move; she didn't need to do a single thing. It was out of her hands now.

'Cat got your tongue, Libby?' he asked. 'It must have. Melbournians hate cats, you better watch out!' He laughed at the football reference. He pushed the balaclava into the inside pocket of his thick black leather coat. He reached for her shoulder with a gloved hand. She shrank backwards, looking down at the ground to avoid any further eye contact.

'What's going on Libby? You wanted this crap to end. You wanted me back. I'm here ... what are you up to?' he said.

The cocking of the pistol fell into the silence between them. Hopkins opened his eyes wide, the whites clear in the moonlight as Anthony's bulk emerged from around the corner of the kiosk. Libby went to his side.

'You've come to the end, mate,' Anthony said. 'There's no way back, no way out. You're dead. You wouldn't take the hint, would you?'

'Stop it, Anthony. Just shoot him. Kill the bastard now!' Libby screamed.

It was enough to distract Anthony's focus and for Hopkins to jump to the ground in a flash and, in almost the same motion, roll under the white guard railing. A shot rang out, almost at the same time as his body cleared the boards and left the pier. The sound of a splash came a split second afterwards.

Libby woke suddenly, startled by the sound of a swimmer hitting the water. She'd been asleep in the late afternoon sun, under the trees at the Manly Swim Centre. She looked around quickly; it was late, turning cool. She remembered what her subconscious mind had just conjured up. It was crushing to find herself back in real life, a reality without hope, another night ahead without safety. Even in her dreams, her efforts to eradicate him only ended with his escape.

It's meant to be, you idiot, she thought. He'll always win.

She gathered her towel and bag and left the centre. But this was not Libby's only dream about ending Hopkins' life. She thought about it again and again in her waking hours. Two of her male friends had offered to bash or maim him, to fix the problem once and for all. She even had one offer to find a hitman. She thought about creating a trap in the backyard and torturing him to death. It was tempting, mad, irresistible.

11

A CRY FOR SANITY

It was the longest week of Libby Masters' life. She'd been embarrassed in front of those closest to her. The few who'd been prepared to support her claims and back her every move now had every reason to rethink their solidarity. No one knew what to believe, including Libby. Her paranoia was growing. Even at work, she felt underlying resentment and disbelief from those she dealt with, though most were ignorant of her trials. Her confidence was at a terrible low and her parents would no longer discuss her plight.

How Hopkins had falsified Telstra traces—or had someone falsify them for him—Libby could only wonder. She knew one important fact, however, it was not she who phoned Hopkins from her home that night or any other night. No amount of paranoia or courtroom trauma was going to colour the truth in her own mind. These were fabricated calls aimed at covering the stalker's alibi, or worse, were strictly designed to entrap his victim before the courts.

Fortunately, Libby was not quite the only one prepared to conceive of either possibility. Whether it was because of an emotional connection to her or a genuine sense of what Hopkins was capable of, Libby's friend Shane was still backing her. He knew Libby could never practise the deception she was accused of and he never gave up suggesting avenues that might be open to them. After all, Libby was not only attempting to survive anymore, she had to clear her name, to do everything in her power to defeat her nemesis.

'I have a friend, Libby, who has a husband in the media and I think it's time to consider making this whole thing public,' urged Shane.

Libby hadn't spoken to anyone, let alone left the sanctity of her parents' home to socialise, even on a Saturday night. Hopkins had not returned for an entire week. She was beginning to let herself hope that he'd stopped, at least for a while. She felt safe enough to dine out at a dimly lit Thai restaurant, situated in a newly-restored terrace at Manly.

Libby had mixed feelings towards Shane's idea. She feared being revealed publicly as a pitiful victim. How would she show her face? What kind of loonies would it bring out of the woodwork? Would it encourage him to return? And what if her boss felt it would damage her relationship with clients? On the positive side of the ledger, she instantly recalled Hopkins' family's reaction to the prospect of any exposure of their son's crimes. Simone had used this prospect with some success on Phillip's mother Kathryn.

Shane's logic made sense: have a story publicised which not would leave any identifiable trace. They guessed a deal could be arranged to ensure that Libby remained anonymous. Shane wanted her to place pressure on Phillip's family and the police and to make some of her own circle of friends think again about whether Libby was telling the truth; but did she need to say who she really was? She could see where he was coming from, but still she wasn't sure.

Then a high-pitched crash pierced the din of the restaurant. One of the front concertina doors had been shattered by a large rock flying across the room, narrowly missing another couple, before landing at the foot of Libby's chair. She seemed to be the only patron who sat unmoved and unsurprised. She knew who'd thrown the rock and remained motionless, staring directly at the shattered window.

'Get this friend of yours to call me tomorrow morning, Shane. We'll do that story,' she said calmly. 'I have to do that story or go out and kill him—one or the other. We'll try this first.'

Shane sensed Libby's blunt and cool demeanour and wasn't about to argue.

The next morning, she was woken by a heavy knock at the front door. She peered through bleary eyes at the clock. It was 6 a.m. and she suspected it was finally the police answering her call from the previous night. She opened the door. In front of her was a young constable, who came straight to the point.

'Sorry it took so long Ms Masters, but we were busy at Manly last night and I'm not so sure we'll be of any use to you anyway.'

Libby was firing in the dark and knew it. She'd been accused of harassing Hopkins, but knew the home phone was faulty and knew the answer could be found in the house somewhere. Only a discovery by the police could make her suspicions stick.

He didn't quite know what he was looking for but followed the Telstra cabling as it weaved in and out, up and down between the skirting boards. It led to below floor level. At Libby's insistence he headed under the house. Only five minutes later he was back, knocking gently at Libby's back door.

'You have faulty phones all right. Are there any clever teenagers in the street?' he asked.

'No, none that I know anyway.'

'Well someone's been tampering with your line and could have been making calls on your account from under the house, I think. You'll need to confirm this.'

The officer had discovered a junction box taped around the power cables with plastic tape. It was a homemade contraption for splitting the one line that ran into and out of the house to create an extension. It was attached to the phone line by two crimp fasteners at either end. The junction box had no official telecommunications markings— it had clearly not been installed by a Telstra technician. Homemade it might have been, but was perfectly adequate for someone to connect a telephone and make any number of calls out, under the Masters' phone account. Whoever had done this had hacked into their phone line; they could listen to any calls made by or received from the house.

Libby, the police and the court had walked right into Hopkins' trap. Libby immediately set about finding a Telstra technician to prove what had happened. It was essential that at any future court hearing the truth be told and her reputation restored. It was as important to her as ridding Hopkins from her life.

'No need for names at all, Libby,' said the journalist on the the telephone. 'We shouldn't be putting victims through that very public experience anyway. It's not a good look and the point can still be made without identification,' he said.

Matt Condon wrote for *The Sun Herald*, a senior features writer who had been introduced to Libby through Shane. He was quite taken by Libby's plight. Her identity would be hidden; but her story would now be out there. Hopkins' name too had to be disguised because, as Condon explained, these were all allegations that no editor would back now that the courts had found in the stalker's favour.

'This is a chance to highlight the inadequacies of stalking legislation and AVOs too. You're not the first woman to feel let down by the system.' Condon's angle was obvious and, although Libby didn't know where it would lead, it was a way of striking back publicly and made her feel empowered. It was at least a start.

'Charmed and Dangerous' read the headline in the Extra features section of the Sunday 16 June 1996 Sydney newspaper. It was the story of a couple: John and Paula. The subheading read 'John's attraction to Paula became a terrifying obsession. Matt Condon reports on the evil menace of stalking.' The article began with a description of the night Libby met Phillip: 'I was attracted to him. He seemed very intense, very intelligent.'

Condon described how Hopkins and Libby went to her home on the lower North Shore. 'I couldn't make a judgement about him that night. He was very quiet, but I knew he was interested in me. He asked a lot of questions but surrendered very little about himself, only that he was involved in computers.'

Condon gave accounts of some of Hopkins' first dysfunctional visits:

> I'd cooked dinner one night and he didn't turn up on time. I didn't think he was coming over so I went to bed. Then he arrived at 10pm. He was obviously drunk. When I asked him to leave he refused to go. He talked his way into staying. It became full-on from that day.

The article continued:

> Although she was unaware of it at the time, Paula was about to enter every woman's nightmare—a nightmare that, despite John's continued breach of charge conditions against him—continues. John is a stalker … She said John began pressuring her for sex at all hours of the night and would go into rages if she rejected his advances.
>
> He would keep me up until 5am arguing with me. He wouldn't leave my house until I caved in. After about three months he started getting physically abusive. He spat on me. He pushed me around. My work began to suffer and people started asking why I looked so tired and run-down. But he had this limitless energy. He would be arguing until 5am and get up at 7am and go off to work.

Condon wrote of the episode involving the discovery of a cut house key:

> One of the most chilling aspects to the relationship was revealed near the end. Paula noticed that her spare house key was missing. It reappeared two days later. Paula had learned that John had cut his own key and had been letting himself into her house at will.
>
> 'It was driving me insane,' she said. 'He would follow me everywhere. He would climb onto the roof of a restaurant and watch me having dinner in another restaurant across the road. He began turning up everywhere I went. I thought initially it was just a coincidence. I've only realised now that he was probably following me daily from about a week after we met. I tried to break up with him but it was impossible.

'I noticed he had a private investigator's handbook in his flat, but I didn't put it all together at the time. On the first night that I finally tried to end it properly he ripped my dress. I tried to call the police, but he wouldn't let me. He pushed me down on the bed and put his hand across my mouth.

There was a brief rundown of his arrest for assaulting Libby and the bizarre attempts to get her back:

Paula moved to her parent's home. She was inundated with flowers, letters and phone calls from John, trying to get her back. He left letters on her office desk before she arrived at work. Four days after being charged he breached his bail conditions by approaching Paula. He was subsequently charged under the State Government's stalking legislation that resulted from the death of Andrea Patrick in Harbord on August 19, 1993. She was killed by her former partner, who later committed suicide. The offence carries a penalty of two years' imprisonment and/or a $5,000 fine.

He quoted Libby:

John approached me, in breach of the stalking charge, at least 30 times since he was charged. The law means nothing. It gets to the point where I'm embarrassed to call the police. I go to bed at night and hear noises and it's him at my bedroom window. He tampered with evidence relating to my parent's telephone line so he could say in court that it was me who had been harassing him. I now have a one-year restraining order against him which stems from the initial assault charge, and it means nothing to him. If I go to see my friend, he's watching me in the backyard. Wherever I go he turns up. I'm constantly on edge. I'm always looking over my shoulder. He has breached his conditions so many times. It's very hard to actually catch him in the act. He has to be dealt with and made aware you cannot do this sort of thing.

The article even touched upon Simone Crowe's experience: 'Paula's problems were exacerbated when she discovered recently that John had stalked a previous girlfriend for more than eight years.'

Condon had done his best to draw in to the case all the relevant authorities, to put the job of protecting Libby into as many laps as possible. He wrote: 'In desperation, Paula has now contacted her local member, Federal MP for Warringah, Tony Abbott. Mr Abbott has contacted the relevant police and says he will ensure Paula's case is not taken lightly.'

Abbott himself was quoted as saying: 'It's horrific. As far as the person being harassed is concerned, their whole life is blighted by this. But how much can the police do in these circumstances? It is one of life's ghastly imponderables.'

Condon also probed for comment from the State Government Attorney-General's office:

The legislation can't stop everything. She should not be afraid to report every incident where he breaches his conditions. It's an enforcement question, that's the job of the police. If he has not paid attention to an order imposed on him by a court, a judge or magistrate would have to sort out the appropriate penalty.

Condon's feature article concluded thus:

Last Saturday night Paula was out at a restaurant dining with a friend. During the evening a rock was thrown, cracking the restaurant window. She has no doubt it was John. Paula said, 'I just wonder if it's ever going to end … I just wish I'd never met him that night … I wish I'd never laid eyes on him.'

When the story was published that Sunday, Libby couldn't wait for the paperboy to come to her street. She purchased the early edition from the local 24-hour convenience shop at 5am and, although it seemed like someone had taken out most of what she'd told Condon, it didn't really matter. The key incidents were there.

It was as though she was reading someone else's nightmare, not her own. And while she felt chilled at what the outcome of the piece might be, she again felt empowered by a great sense of revenge. It didn't undo the untruths told and the prolonged pain of his stalking, but she knew it would straighten a few misconceptions among those she knew.

The publicity from the article would certainly make the police a tad more receptive—which she knew had to happen if Hopkins was ever going to be forced to answer for his deeds. That was the scenario she dreamed of, but at least for now, she was confident enough to contemplate such a result.

'Hello, Libby. This is Matt here. How are you?' came the voice at the other end of the telephone that afternoon. Matt's call was one of at least twenty that day, the others being from friends and family who had cottoned on to the link between the published story and Libby's. Caller after caller had congratulated her on upstaging her predator and putting the pressure back on those who'd let her down. But this call was different. Matt felt for Libby and had been working on empowering her further. He was about to step things up a notch—move her towards the endgame she envisaged.

'I've got a friend, Libby, another journalist, who I've been talking to about your case this week. And he's very interested in helping. But you'll need to meet with him, talk about what he's got in mind and make a decision.'

'Why would that be such a big deal, Matt? I got through the story with you easily. It came out great. The Hopkins family has obviously read it, and Phillip will be watched like a hawk from here on surely. And if I need the cops, they've got politicians everywhere waiting to catch them out if they appear slack. What are you talking about?'

'*A Current Affair* wants to film Phillip in the dark, catch him out, with your help. And it could put him away, Libby. It could lead to the end. This is powerful media.'

There was a long pause. Libby cleared her throat, stunned, frightened at the prospect of television involvement.

'I'm not sure. How will it work?'

'Can I just suggest you meet him? He's a very close friend and knows his stuff. But he also takes good care of those who find themselves in trouble. Meet him and then decide, okay?'

'Okay. I will. I've come this far. What's his number?'

12

PRIME TIME

This is where I, the author of this book, come into Libby's story. I was a senior producer with *A Current Affair*, a bit of an old hand, having spent most of my professional life reporting. She was supremely apprehensive about going further, but her confidence in Matt had persuaded her to take another step. She agreed to meet me and reporter Jane Hansen at a restaurant in East Sydney. It was not a location likely to attract her stalker's attention. It was more a typical posh spot for two journalists to ply their trade.

Libby was curious to find out what more could be done, knowing that she needed to make a decision while the story was hot. I made my credentials clear from the start and thought it appropriate to mention the fact that I'd won journalistic awards for past coverage of current affairs and news. I had been following Libby's case, spending many hours with my friend Matt discussing the story and what my program might be able to prove. Matt's description of Libby's plight was a real eye-opener. Her story was custom-made for a reality-style surveillance operation, in which our hidden cameras could be used to track Hopkins' suspicious movements.

This was my specialty. Two years earlier I recorded a police officer extorting cash from a petty thief in Kempsey. The money had allegedly been to pay off a magistrate, but it was an elaborate con job perpetrated by a senior NSW detective to line his own pockets. Our team had placed a small lipstick camera in the stalk of a house plant in the lounge room of the petty thief, which would record the cash changing hands. An audio recording of the meeting, albeit illegally obtained via a small FM microphone in the rear of the pillows on the thief's lounge, enabled us to monitor whether the bribe was paid and received—and whether it was worth pouncing. Once confirmation was broadcast from the house, we 'walked in' on the detective in the front yard of the house, confronting him over his extraction of dirty money. There was more than enough proof against the detective, who was later sentenced to six months in prison.

This project would be an adaptation of the same assignment and might even deliver Libby her own conviction. There were clearly more variables to consider in this case, but I was confident something equally dramatic and effective could be achieved. Libby took us through the ins and outs of her case against Hopkins and talked about the dead ends she'd encountered with the private investigator and the police. I preferred to take a shotgun approach to following Hopkins, whom I didn't underestimate for a second. Our plan was to use infra-red surveillance on the exterior of the Masters' home, bring in Libby's private investigator—who'd already done extensive work on Hopkins—and take a cooperative approach with police once we'd recorded enough evidence of the stalker's presence to jam them into a corner. If the story had legs and was likely to be aired, the police simply couldn't ignore it.

'We'll go all out with this bastard, Libby,' I told her. 'With our program involved, you'll find that the police will take a completely different approach to your situation. I reckon it's a fair bet that the local detectives will be instructed from above to get onto the case and solve it. They won't want to be embarrassed by this, Libby. We can't promise that part of it, but we are very confident.'

'But can footage of an unidentified, balaclava-ed stalker, place Phillip at the scene?'

'The visual evidence gets the cops involved in a far more wholehearted way. They will smother this joint before he arrives again. You just watch. I'm prepared to stay at your house overnight for a week to record the evidence. We won't leave you in the lurch—we'll get him. And I feel lucky about it too, which helps.'

I always felt it healthy to be a little cocky in front of 'story talent'. I needed to exude an air of motivation and hope. Libby knew a hard sell when she saw it though. No matter how enthusiastic I was to score the big story, I sensed that she was ever doubtful. But she had little choice. How else was she going to end this? Nothing else had sent him away.

Jane was far more sympathetic, as only a woman could be. They bonded instantly, and gradually Libby came round to the idea of going ahead with our plans.

'What about my face—can you disguise it? Can you use a different name?'

I knew that this would be a crucial point in swaying her. But I also knew that to garner the kind of personal sympathy for the story required in a lengthy piece of television, we needed her face on the box. I needed her to tell her own story, face to camera. I was prepared to change her name if need be, but only to appease her doubts. It would make little difference if her face was beamed to a national television audience.

'We need you. We need your face and your story. We need the empathy to make it stick with the audience. If we get that, we create pressure on authorities. Without it, there's no killer punch.'

'I don't know whether I could do that. I could lose my job, I could damage everything.'

'Damage everything? He's done that already, Libby.' I knew this was crunch time. Without a real person for the audience to relate to, a genuine victim, the story would lose a great deal in the telling, not to mention credibility. I leaned forward. This next minute was crucial—I was determined to return to the office with a green light on a potentially powerful story. But at the same time, I was genuinely moved by Libby's plight and wanted to free her from this tyranny. She didn't have a life. 'As for your job, by the sound of it, you're on the brink of losing it anyway,' I said. 'Your boss would welcome a woman with guts and courage putting her life back on track and not allowing herself to be dictated to by a lunatic. Imagine the support you'd have if things go well. If not, you'll have understanding beyond anything you have now. You can't lose.'

'What about Phillip? If he knows you're here and he doesn't front, you give up and I'm left to fend off a maniac racked by feelings of revenge. That's not my idea of winning, Chris.'

'The vision, the public exposure and the police attention are the greatest personal insurance policy you could ever have. If anything happens to you, anything, they have one suspect and a mile of pressure to build a case. I have never exposed a victim to greater danger. I have never had someone we've interviewed before targeted by those they accuse. I've done this for over a decade.'

Libby paused, trapped by our solutions to her dilemma. She was concerned that any story would adversely impact on the upcoming case of assault against Hopkins. We both reluctantly assured her that we would not run any story prior to the hearing of his case.

It was an empty promise, because not even our legal advisors would warn us off running a story before an assault case in a lower court without a jury. I wasn't prepared to jeopardise the story by having to explain the legal realities.

I'd rolled out all the compelling arguments I could think of. It was time to back off, to let all of it sink in. I could see Libby's need to be saved, to be protected, and felt we'd done enough to get her over the line. She was clearly nervous, but couldn't argue with what we had put to her. She sat back in her chair and the tension of the debate suddenly eased. We suddenly looked at each other differently. I was standing in her shoes, saw her torment. I was fired up about the prospect of catching her predator, but I could sense that she wanted to make the most of that sentiment too. She could see how determined we were to nail Hopkins. She smiled, realising that there was really no decision to make. It was time to load up and fire back. *A Current Affair* was the perfect vehicle for that.

'Let's get him—once and for all. I'm exhausted, Chris. I can't take this any more.'

'Excellent,' I replied in a state of subdued relief, 'time to stalk the stalker.'

We were set to go into overdrive. Jane told her the team would be back the following morning with engineers and all the techno-geeks the story required. As we said goodbye I gently took Libby by the shoulders.

'Thank you. If he wants to harass you again, we'll be here and we'll nail him for you. I can't think of any greater pleasure.'

I asked a couple of logistical questions about windows and eaves and whether the sensor lights had been installed at her home and checked by a professional. These were obvious tools for nighttime surveillance and had to be functioning properly. Libby told me that they were purchased and assembled by her father and that they didn't always trigger as expected. I told her that a lighting fellow would be calling first thing the next morning too. We needed the sensors to trigger at the very last moment, not tipping Hopkins off.

We put Libby into a cab and began what turned out to be one of the most exciting investigations we'd undertaken.

I headed back to my car, mobile phone in one hand, notepad in the other. I was already talking to unit managers, crews and producers before I'd got the engine started. I felt that Libby was recharged by our enthusiasm, that we had given her hope.

The very next morning, I arrived with a team of cameramen, sound recordists and engineers to begin the technical set up of Libby's home for the first surveillance operation to be carried out that night. We also called the corporate division of Telstra. I had a close senior contact there and twisted some arms to get an authorised technician out to verify what the constable had found—that the Masters' phone line had been tampered with. It didn't take long for the technician to come to the same conclusion: the cables had been split, an old junction box attached and crimps used to attach an extension. Calls could be made from underneath Libby's floorboards, under her very feet, without her having an inkling of what was going on.

She was now equipped with knock-out evidence of Hopkins' dirty work. The tampering could not be proven to be his doing, but for the purposes of a national current affairs story, the case against Libby's oppressor had begun. The circumstantial evidence, along with Libby's allegations and whatever was caught on camera was certainly enough to prosecute on television.

'We don't say a single thing about this just yet,' I warned. 'I'll ensure that both your installer and this Telstra technician lodge full reports and make affidavits on this. You sit down and write what you've seen too. I'll take some snaps and we'll sit tight for now.'

Libby was miffed at the secrecy. She wondered why this evidence wasn't good enough in itself to be taken to the police and acted upon. But we had the bigger picture in mind. 'Libby, possibly proving that he tampered with your phones and did actually breach his AVO—and I think you'll still have trouble making the link—is going to get you zilch,' I explained quietly, so no one else in the room could hear. 'We have to compile a whole brief of evidence to get the police interested and have a case good enough to air. Leave this in my hands and stop worrying. We're on our way.'

We were on our way alright. The team spent the best part of half a day on the property bringing in stainless steel cases, unpacking tiny monitors and kilometres of cable. There were small videotapes, light boxes, hefty video cameras and tripods and even gardening equipment used to remove certain branches and bushes in the backyard. As well as additional sensor lights, the team had attached small infra-red cameras to the sensor light brackets. They were almost invisible and certainly would be in the dark. Four of them had been carefully attached to cables that were threaded up onto the gutter of the house and inside the downpipes. For each of the cameras, hardly two centimetres of cable was visible. It was a clever bit of work.

Libby stood and stared at the shiny black face of one of the cameras, marvelling at what it might see. In spite of their tiny size, the cameras looked highly intimidating. Libby's remembered reading 1984 at school with its visions of Big Brother. In this case, the threat of visual invasion was working for her.

By late afternoon, Libby's sunroom looked like a television studio; her bedroom a mini television control room. Everywhere you walked there was a cable or box to trip over.

'I'd like to roll on a master interview tonight if we can, Libby,' I said, in a deliberately laid-back way, so as not to frighten her. It was actually the hardest thing Libby would face for us: a probing, exhausting interview on camera.

Libby was reluctant, but she had little option if she wanted her story to be told. The team was in place, the producers had assigned a reporter who was en route and, as I explained, we were ready to lay the foundation story before the surveillance began. By seven-thirty Libby found herself sitting on the couch, which had been dragged at an angle across the room, vicious lights glaring at her from both sides and Jane Hansen in a chair opposite, waiting for the nod.

'Camera's rolling, Jane,' instructed the cameraman.

Over the space of 45 minutes, Libby retraced her life, firstly pre-Phillip, then through their early passionate days together and into the seedy world of being stalked incessantly. She seemed at ease after several minutes. On a couple of occasions she paused to hold herself back from crying. Reliving the moments of terror and abuse was hard enough to get through, let alone expressing it clearly for the millions who would see this. Jane was a highly experienced operator who handled her sensitively. I watched the interview at close-hand, sitting nearby on a large stainless steel box.

'That's all I've got; I think we've got it all,' Jane eventually said quietly.

The interview was over. Libby was, in television current affairs terms, amazing talent. Her story was riveting, her sincerity compelling and both Jane Hansen and myself knew that we had a key piece of the puzzle 'in the can'. Jane wanted some additional filming done in the backyard, which was a smart move. Libby's explanation of where his balaclava would appear even had the crew's skin crawling. Jane left soon afterwards, as did several of the crew, quietly excited by what they'd accomplished and having shown great empathy for Libby and her plight. She was at home with this mob of enthusiastic and professional media strangers. She'd heard all the stories about how conniving the media was, especially the commercial television sector, but so far, she felt she was in good hands.

Three of the crew remained in Libby's house that night. After a quick scoff of fast food, the diet of a surveillance producer, I took over Libby's bedroom, which had no less than four television monitors packed together on the floor next to her bed. Cables led from these to a large multiple recording unit hidden in the wardrobe. There was a pile of opened videotapes next to the unit and another pile of brick-like batteries with a large charger next to them. A small stool was positioned directly in front of the monitors, which was where I planned to sit. We asked Libby to stay in the dimly lit lounge room, watching television, to play bait to Hopkins. Meanwhile, my job was fairly simple: watch the bank of screens, quietly reload tapes and batteries, but mostly sit in wait.

The infra-red camera lit up the backyard on my screen as if it was the middle of the day. The pictures were grainy but provided superb contrast. Even the slight swaying of Cocos palms in a tiny breeze on the southern fence was easily detected. Yet, outside, to the naked eye, it was pitch dark, not a breath, not a movement. In fact, the area surrounding Libby's parents' home was an extremely dark place. As a well-established old Northern Beaches suburb, there were high gum trees adorning the boundaries, thick bushes in between and, being 200-odd metres away from the nearest arterial road, the area was not well lit by street lights. It was a very dark pocket of Balgowlah and, as such, a stalker's paradise. This was extremely scary territory for anyone on the receiving end of such treatment.

The first night was an exciting operation, despite long periods of nothing, not even an inkling of company. The mobile crew two blocks away performed two-way radio tests with me. They were parked nearby, waiting for the call to either head Hopkins off in a getaway street, or head back to Libby's house to record his movements on the property. At one stage I ventured out in the dark along the side of the house to adjust the position of one of the infra-red cameras with a broom. After several hours Libby and I started talking about Hopkins, why she thought he was the way he was. I was constantly keeping Libby focused on what would happen if he did turn up, how the team would react. It was important she not give the game away. Alerting Hopkins to the trap would keep him away until we were long gone.

By 4am, with no sign of Hopkins, I asked her if there was any clear pattern to Hopkins' stalking. She made somewhat of a sobering observation. 'You know, he hasn't actually been here for two weeks. Not since the last court case,' she whispered from the lounge room.

I froze, and didn't reply immediately. I was not only genuinely keen to catch Hopkins in the act, I was also under considerable pressure to obtain some good footage as well. My boss had given me just five days with so much technology and manpower tied up on one story, in one location. We needed results and this was not what I needed to hear. Somehow we hadn't discussed this point. Her stories of stalking and harassment had seemed so fresh.

Night two dragged on without a whisper until a mangy cat jumped the fence and into the line of sight of the rear infra-red camera, startling me almost off my stool. It was a good drill and proved the set-up worked.

Meanwhile our conversations between the bedroom and the lounge room were more frequent, less whispered and meandered from television politics and office romances to the occasional giggling fit about what some of the station's more public figures got up to in their dressing rooms. Libby knew I was embellishing the gossip, but it sure alleviated the boredom of sitting around staring at nothing for hours on end.

There was always the danger that this might turn from one of my more exciting assignments into an empty roll of static pictures—not a story in sight. Towards the end of night two, I was getting nervous. Had Hopkins detected us? But how? Or worse still, had this serious case of stalking fizzled out into a fabrication? Was Libby just hanging on to the story to save face?

Night three saw a change in tactics. We turned up well before dark, before regular work hours had ended. It was an attempt to avoid any possibility of being seen entering the property during the afternoon. Hopkins may have been watching the street and noticed that Libby had company. The crew too no longer roamed the nearby streets. Although the crew car was unmarked, its mere presence might have been a give-away. The crew now had to sit in wait in the dirty, dark shed in the backyard. It wasn't a popular strategy, but it made sense. And to complete the change in tactics, Libby would move from room to room, more like she would if it was a normal night. Her lengthy presence in the one room may have looked out of place, possibly staged.

The set of changes brought results, but not the ones we hoped for. At 2:40am, as I sipped on yet another Diet Coke to keep myself from dozing off, a sharp flash of light appeared between two bushes in the south-west corner of the property. It spiked me into action, my eyes wide open, my first sign of trouble in three nights. I feared it might be wishful thinking, conjuring false images through boredom.

'Libby,' I whispered. 'I think we've got company. I've got him!'

Then camera three picked up a second flash at the back fence. It became a beam for a few moments and then went out. I waited and waited for more, for any sign of movement or light; there was none. What Hopkins was up to, if it was indeed him, was uncertain. The fact that he was willing to come to the property, risk being caught—if he had indeed suspected something over the two earlier nights—and now left without any satisfaction or response, was baffling. He was always prepared to do his homework, always patient enough to wait until the time was right. He was a perfectionist and what I'd now discovered was that, if he sniffed something was not right, he was also prepared to simply turn around and walk away.

Night four arrived and it was the top of the ninth, so to speak. We didn't want to leave ourselves just one last night to hook the target. The odds of scoring on the final night were low indeed. I had to make it happen; I had to find an edge.

During one of our lengthy, middle of the night whispered conversations from bedroom to lounge, Libby had told me about her private investigator and how he'd been given the run-around, unable to get too far late at night. He did of course provide witness to Hopkins' breach of AVO, but this too had worked out badly for Libby. While this PI may not have scored a direct hit, I could still use an extra set of eyes. He had some knowledge and history of the site and our target, if he could be convinced to help out. So for night four, Rob Hearn was employed as part of surveillance.

Hearn would be on foot. While he'd never found Hopkins' launch spot, he did have his suspicions about three locations nearby. His role was to comb all three alternately for the duration of the evening. He was in two-way radio contact with myself and the crew. We could now monitor places previously out-of-bounds to us.

It was early on night four when the two-way crackled with a calm message from Hearn: 'Sighted what could be a target ... heading through laneway up ahead, in your direction.'

Again I was startled by Hopkins' behaviour. He'd come so early, after three nights of virtually nothing.

'You know it's him?' I asked.

'Not sure,' replied Hearn. 'But he's definitely acting suspicious and I'll try to keep up with him.'

'No. Stay away. Come to the other side of this location to watch for his departure that way. The crew will be there at the back if we need them.'

I was attempting to cover all bases and, if this was to be a short flashlight visit, I didn't want to frighten Hopkins away. Right on cue, Hopkins flashed his light across the backyard from the back fence. The crew in the shed had their two-way receiver connected to an earpiece so that the crackle of the hand-held unit didn't alert Hopkins to their presence.

'Should we get out of here and nail him?' asked the cameraman.

'Stay put you blokes,' I warned. 'We need more than a shaky picture of a shadowy bloke running over a fence a mile away ... hold your positions.'

The adrenalin was pumping among the entire crew. This time, we told Libby nothing about what we'd seen. On our previous sighting of his flashlight, I suspected that Libby's minute physical reaction to the news might have been enough to tip him off. It was only a possibility, but with just one-and-a-half nights left on the clock, I was determined not to take even the slightest chance.

'I have the torch in frame,' I told the others. 'Only the torch, so wait on.'

The torch soon went out. There was nothing for an excruciating twenty minutes until one of the monitors detected a flying object. A soccer ball had been catapulted from behind the fence—flying over into the rear yard—one of his favourite tricks. It bounced and triggered one of the sensor lights.

'He's smart, you blokes,' Libby whispered. 'He's working out where he can approach without the detectors going off. Watch out.'

Fifteen seconds later there was a huge crash, like something had hit the side of the house. He'd shifted location to an adjoining property and had thrown what sounded like a plant pot at the wall. The impact was quite close to Libby's room, where we'd positioned all the monitoring equipment. This time though the sensor didn't trigger. Libby was no longer in the lounge area but had made her way to the kitchen after the first missile, the ball, had been thrown. I didn't want Libby's demeanour to tip him off or dissuade him from entering the property. We moved her away from the rear sliding doors and her parents were told to remain at the front of the house, in their bedroom, no matter what they heard happening at the rear.

Then, a series of objects was thrown towards the back veranda. These were lemons from a neighbour's tree and, after three hit and ricocheted from the veranda railings, the sensor lights were finally triggered. Hopkins seemed to be roughly plotting the shadow points in the yard for a possible entry. Suddenly I was blinded by a direct beam of light from his wandering torch, which had shone in the face of one of our infra-red lenses. Night had not just turned into day, it had whitewashed the screen, as if Hopkins had intended to seek it out. This final explosion of light was the last image to appear on our screens that night. After five minutes of waiting, Hearn's voice came through the two-way.

'I've got a sighting; he's just removed a balaclava and he's hiking it across Sydney Road. I knew this was where he was entering the block. Might have him nailed.'

Hearn had been following the shooting gallery hi-jinx but was not prepared to keep guard at the front of the property. From the rear of the home, he was banking on sighting Hopkins at a point about half a kilometre in a direct line west from where he'd been throwing his missiles. This was where Hearn had always suspected was the launching spot. But he was on foot and well behind his target.

'I'm still a hundred away, I'll try and catch up,' Hearn told us.

'Don't let him see you though, mate,' I replied. 'We need him back.'

He didn't reach Hopkins in time. He'd crossed the road and run through a block of apartments that had a public walk-through archway leading into another street. If he had a vehicle there, it was gone. But this was definitely one of his launch spots. We now knew his entry and exit methods, although we had no visual recording of his movements.

The night was not a total failure; the clear recordings of torch light on the property added to our growing pile of visual material. It was certainly suspenseful, even on tape. It was heart-pounding work for all of us, seeing this flash of light in pitch darkness, imagining his departure through heavy bush and over several fences. Not a normal day at the office for sure. And Hearn's work was vital. We now had an opportunity to follow Hopkins and trap him. But why was he running? There was no one on his tail when he left the property and his frantic sprint across the road had begun well before Hearn had entered the same road. He was in a hurry, which could not possibly have been related to what had gone on in the backyard. Again Hopkins actions were puzzling, unless of course, he had busted the operation with one laser-like beam from his torch.

As the crew packed up that night, there weren't too many words spoken. The pressure was well and truly on. The program's bosses were not throwing any further technical and human resources into the story— not even for one extra night. There had been an attempt back at the office by those who weren't involved in the assignment to cast doubt on Libby's motives and have the story shelved. It was motivated by jealousy and was nothing new in the competitive game of commercial current affairs. My attempt to bleed an extension from the program's executive ranks only highlighted to them how improbable it was that we could track down the stalker. One senior producer even accused Libby of being a 'loop' and wanted the story wrapped up, written and edited as a small news-sized story. My fiery reaction to the idea was enough to quell the argument. But the Balgowlah project had just one final evening to find the man and prove the premise. We had one final roll of the die to come. I was still cocky enough to think we could do it, an assertion based in bravado rather than common sense.

13

LAST ROLL

The tactics would remain almost the same—after all, there were few other options available. There was one change; equipped with our knowledge of Hopkins' exit route, the camera crew was back in their car and stationed a block away, waiting for the call to head off Hopkins after his visit. Libby and I were the only ones in the house this time, both the crew and investigator had to be mobile.

As the crew arrived to set up about two hours before dark, as tapes and batteries were lined up for the last time, I tried to imbue the others with a feeling of hope. We needed luck and, at the very least, we were doing everything in our power to make that luck. I told Libby and the crew that I was certain that the previous night's shenanigans were a prelude for a proper attempt by Hopkins to get closer to his target. We shouldn't be put off by his premature departure. I felt it had nothing to do with our presence. I suspected he was a quite a busy boy. We'd done all the preparation anyone could do in the circumstances and I felt confident we could film our man up close. Even without perfect identification, if he did front and was brazen enough to get in full view of the infra-red cameras, the show would have its story and the momentum to take it to the next level.

On that final night of filming, no one had much to say. We knew our roles. The crew was in position even before Libby arrived home, just before dark. She was feeling uneasy about all the trouble the program had gone to, based on her say so, without a result. She was nowhere near as confident as we were.

We made a fruitless start. I sat staring intently at the four monitors in front of me. My back ached from a week perched on this wretched stool as

I rotated my head and massaged my own neck. My eyes were red and sore as the hour grew later and later. Not a single movement or sound. The optimism was slowly sapping out of me ... until just before 1am.

'Target is crossing Sydney Road, Chris,' Hearn reported from within sight of the apartment building, Hopkins' launching spot. Our perseverance might just pay off. Our man was in the neighbourhood and calling! He was on his way, into the trap which had been set and refined each night this week. My heart was now pumping rapidly. His arrival, signalled by flashlight, came at precisely 1am. Libby's lounge lights were on and she was lying on the couch, having long since nodded off to sleep. The sight of his waving torch, the knowledge that this was the final chance, brought enormous nervous tension. It was absolutely black outside; cloud cover hid the quarter moon and the whole precinct looked as if it had been subject to a blackout. The now familiar torch act carried on for ten long minutes. I didn't dare blink an eyelid. I also didn't wish to wake Libby with news of his presence. That would give the game away completely. Her sleeping might be just what we needed to provoke him. The bait was set.

Then the lightshow disappeared, and I was faced with the same old static shot of the back fence. Don't you dare leave, I urged him silently. A split second after the light went out, my screen was filled with a threatening balaclava emerging from the darkness above the back fence. In one sharp movement his eyes rose above the fence, detached, floating. They held me frozen like a statue. Then, seconds later, his body appeared, scaling the fence and landing in a crouched, cat-like position in the corner of the yard. It was surreal and utterly frightening. He was now on the property.

I had my story; the rest, wherever that was now heading, would be a bonus. A sense of great relief flushed through my body. That grainy infra-red shot of those wide eyes peering starkly from his black mask, had been a terrifying sight—more terrifying than I'd ever imagined. My heart was racing in a way I'd never experienced. My breath was shortening as if I'd been winded, and while I was excited to be on the brink of a big story, one we'd waited so long to hook, I was very, very nervous of what was about to unfold in the middle of the night in this dark Balgowlah backyard. We might have been filming the truth, but there was no protection or security at all. The sight of the balaclava reminded me how alone I was. There was no back up, not for what might unfold over the next few minutes.

Hopkins remained in this crouched position at the back fence for what seemed like several minutes. He was indeed a patient predator. Then he jumped up and began walking quickly towards the back of the house. I followed his movements through camera three, as he'd walked out of sight of the wide shot camera trained on the back fence. Hopkins walked right up to the railing of the veranda and sighted Libby through the sliding doors. He wanted a closer look. It seemed to me that in a very primitive way, he tilted his head to get a better sight of her sleeping on the couch. It was a perverse kind of leer. I could see that he was smiling; his eyes began to squint. He began to lift a foot to step up onto the landing. As he did so, one of the new sensor lights was triggered, and he instantly ran back behind the bush on the right-hand side of the yard, half-way down. He had an unusual gait, a kind of uncoordinated jog. It made him look quite vulnerable, although he clearly held the upper hand.

He again crouched, rock steady, his head at a 45-degree angle. He stayed behind the bushes for several minutes before jumping up and heading back away from the house towards the fence, awkwardly sliding over the palings, catching his clothing on the serrated top of the wooden fence. But he was gone and I sighed so heavily, I had to tell myself to shut up. I wondered whether that was it; whether his show had an encore.

I told the crew of what was happening and asked them to head straight to the apartment building, grab their gear and wait for Hopkins to emerge. I turned to the lounge room and tried to wake our sleeping heroine.

'Hey, Libby, wake up. He's been and gone. Libby?' I said quietly, but enough to stir her briefly.

We had our pictures, we had our story and experienced overwhelming relief. I looked at the four blank screens I'd been focused on all week, and pondered as I had done many times the lunacy of his actions. Why would he comb the streets, navigate backyards, risk spiders and injury and don a balaclava in the middle of the night? I sat still, mesmerised, waiting for word from Hearn or the crew. It didn't come. What was happening?

In one terrifying flash, Hopkins burst into view on camera two, which was trained on the side lane of the house, its range extending to the long-leafed tree above the fence. He stood, a frightening colossus on top of the fence, hanging on to the tree like an ape, moving his head to try and see into the slat windows. The sensors did not trigger. He had found another detection shadow by entering the lane from above the fence, not below it. The shock rattled me. My heart was pumping frantically again, having calmed only moments earlier. I was petrified. He was now as close as he'd ever been. Although I'd spoken his name, imagined his character and geared myself up to catch him for so long, he was at that moment, simply an intruder. He could have been any violent armed robber breaking into my own house. It was truly horrifying.

It took me another few seconds to register an even more gruesome reality—Hopkins was standing on the fence, in his intimidating stance, directly outside Libby's bedroom, trying to look into the very room I was now sitting in. This violent lunatic was only three metres from me, if that, and there was no crew outside or on their way. Libby had fallen back to sleep and the realisation of what might be required of me sucked the air from my lungs. I simply could not take the next breath. It was a feeling I'd never experienced before. I crouched, out of his sight I hoped, and turned to look for Libby, but down here, I couldn't see her at all. It didn't really matter because I didn't have the lung capacity to say a single word to her. My heart was now beating louder than any other noise around me. The humming of video machines became a din.

At the very least, I was expecting to be seen and, at worst, Hopkins, within arm's reach of the slat windows at the top of the wall, would attempt to break into the room. It was clear what he intended: to gain entry and scare the living daylights out of his victim. I would have to confront this madman face to face. I was part of the story now, not simply recording it.

I was struggling with my physical state but quickly realised that I had to get further out of sight to avoid being detected. I grabbed for the bed covers and attempted to smother the brightly lit monitors in front of me. They were a dead giveaway. At the same time I rolled partially under the bed and out of sight.

From under the bed, I wriggled myself into position to see the monitor that was capturing Hopkins outside the room. I saw him stretching his neck to get a better view and see whether someone was actually in the room. Then he leaned across the lane to grab for the window slats. His shoulder supported his weight against the external wall of the house while he loosened the slat windows open. It was the first sound of the stalker's movements I had actually heard and it sent a shiver down my spine.

It was now obvious that Hopkins wanted to get inside fast. He was battling to obtain a decent grip on the windows and I thought that his shoes on the fence were slipping. He couldn't keep this up much longer. I prayed that the intruder would be unable to get into this room.

I attempted to warn Libby with a muffled, breathless voice. I was becoming worried about what would happen to her. I could at least put up some kind of resistance. But it was no good. Libby was dead to the world and for once feeling secure enough to fall into a deep sleep. Without yelling, I couldn't do anything about it. Who knew how aggressive Hopkins might become if he knew another male was inside the house? All I could do was send a muffled message to the camera crew. It was perfect timing for them to hit the backyard, camera and lights blazing. The crew picked up the call clearly and signalled that they were on their way.

Hopkins couldn't get in and was about to lose his balance from a dangerous height. It was time to get out of there. He pushed his body against the wall to regain a vertical position with his arms locked onto the tree overhanging the fence. He waited several seconds before jumping down into the yard next door. He was off. I came out from under the bed. I threw the covers off the monitors, and watched the screens to see if Hopkins had gone to another location in the yard. I began breathing heavily as if I'd been in a chase. There was no sign of him at all.

Sixty seconds later the television crew burst down the side of the house from the front, with Hearn in tow. The glare of the camera light shone down the alley and I went out the back doors to greet them.

'You've missed him, he's taken off … but it doesn't matter, we've got our story,' I told the out-of-breath trio. 'He almost made it inside, but he couldn't jemmy the windows in her room. But we've got him; we've got a story and a half, fellas.'

Libby emerged onto the the veranda, looking totally confused. The four of us turned to her and smiled. She looked totally bewildered, but she had so much to be happy about.

'You're about to get rid of this bastard, Libby,' I said, shaking. 'We've got him and the cops will be falling over themselves to get onboard now. He took the bait, the whole bloody lot.'

As well as being thrilled for Libby, I was incredibly relieved that the waiting was over, that our time, energy and fight for resources had been worth it. So much for being busted by one beam of light! Hopkins had no idea what kind of extravagant trap had been set for him.

We returned inside to view the recorded tapes. A few beers were passed around among the troops, and, while it wasn't a boisterous celebration at that time of the morning, we had every reason to celebrate. The startling images backed Libby's story to the hilt. It was evidence that would finally eradicate any inkling of doubt in the minds of her parents, who would later see the images for themselves. Any idea that their daughter had lost her marbles because of her traumatic break-up was now utterly quashed.

With the evidence obtained under the house, Libby's lengthy interview and the frighteningly dramatic images collected over the week, the show had a very powerful story to tell its national audience. Libby was about to be vindicated in the most public way possible. The full impact of her story would turn out to be nothing short of colossal—and not entirely to the script.

'Sensational,' said the executive in charge of special projects at *A Current Affair*. 'Hang onto it. It's a weekend promo. We'll ramp it up big time. Can you film the cops arresting him as a follow-up? That'd be bloody brilliant.'

After living and breathing the commercial news and current affairs genre for almost fifteen years, there was no need to ask for a translation. The story was to be held back from broadcast until the station was able to promote it through their top-rating weekend programs, and run it on the biggest audience night: Monday. This gave us time to get reporter Jane Hansen heavily involved on camera again, both at the scene and one-on-one with Libby, and for us to have one more go at surveillance with police on site.

Depending on how our negotiations went with the local detectives, there was a good chance we could hold them back from arresting Hopkins for now, no matter what happened on the additional night of surveillance. The story was good enough to go as it was. Any further legal activity might stifle what could be reported, weakening a powerful story. The reaction back at the office had been applause, and the whole place was buzzing with what was to come.

There was still work to be done, however. Researchers had to search and mark all the relevant and interesting aspects of the story on tape. Editors began compiling and editing sequences using Libby's interview and the recorded episodes of stalking. Jane began filming segments with Libby at locations where she'd witnessed Hopkins' predatory behaviour and went to work on scripting the story. I started working the phones.

Detective Sergeant Ray Peattie ran the Manly Detectives Unit for more than five years. He was an institution in the area, although I'd heard some quite suspect stories concerning his behaviour—such as favouring some associates and arresting others, who would often lodge complaints against him.

Lines can become blurred in crime-fighting, but how much of what I'd heard was true, I wasn't certain. A friend of mine in the media had experienced a run-in with Peattie first hand, which confirmed to me that Peattie could be used, but not trusted.

I made several phone calls to Peattie, offering him an invitation to join the team for two final surveillance operations. I explained that, unless the police agreed to hold off any arrest until at least the following week, after our first story was likely to air, there'd be no cooperation and, as I intimated, no favourable assessment of police involvement either. Some might call it media blackmail; I was simply protecting what we'd all worked so hard to achieve. It was in Peattie's interests to cooperate; we were handing the opportunity to gather further evidence to him on a plate.

The night after our victory, the television crews and ten plain-clothed officers attached to the Manly Detectives joined forces at Libby's home to see Hopkins in action first hand. If it didn't come off, there was no harm done, but it would provide Peattie with a drill of how our evidence was obtained. Who could tell, Hopkins might have rostered himself on for the night.

If Libby felt her home had been invaded on the nights we'd been there so far, she'd seen it all now. Apart from herself and her parents, there were now a reporter, a producer, two television crew, a private investigator and ten coppers! It was mayhem in the house, despite everyone's attempts to lie low and remain quiet.

Hearn did not sight Hopkins at his usual launching spot, but sure enough, early in the night, there was his torch flashing centimetres above the fence. The previous night's tension-filled atmosphere, when we'd had everything to lose, was replaced by a sense of adventure. With so many mountain-sized men in the house, Libby had absolutely nothing to be scared of. She was actually enjoying all the attention and was intrigued by how the police would react to his appearance. She recognised one of the detectives from an earlier visit. On that occasion he had tut-tutted his way back to the car, questioning Libby's sanity.

Now here was the light. Everyone huddled around the monitors and could see it plainly. The police were impressed with the technology, turning night into day. But the only other sighting came a few minutes after the first flash of the torch. His big round eyes, framed by the balaclava, peered up over the fence. Whether he heard or sensed something or not, he was not entering the property that night. What we did record, however, was a portion of half-eaten pizza that he dropped over the fence into Libby's back yard. It was a macabre calling card.

He was gone in a flash—but where? The call went out to the mobile chasers, but he had vanished into thin air; no launching spot detected, no torch—no stalker. They lay in wait for several more hours, but the night was a fizz. Although the sighting of a mystery torch was enough to bring back the crew one last time. The police bagged the pizza, in case forensic officers could match his bite down the track.

To have a squad of police working on a Friday night was a rare achievement. Hearn was now in his surveillance van, two plain-clothed police officers were circling the block in an unmarked car and the television crew, reporter onboard, were also ducking in and out of nearby streets, all waiting to see where Hopkins would emerge, where he would position his vehicle. Hearn had long suspected that the stalker had been rotating his launching spots; it made sense. Tonight his hunch paid off.

'Got target in sight, he's just run across Sydney Road and over a back fence,' blared the report from the police radio.

They didn't know where he'd parked his car, but they knew where he'd probably return to. The crews, however, were told to hang off and wait until he'd actually reached Libby's house and come back, but they'd given the police at the house excellent forewarning. Within just two minutes the torch appeared in the backyard and he didn't waste any time jumping the fence.

As the four officers positioned in the house began unlocking the back doors to arrest Hopkins, the stalker did an about-turn, and like a panther, sprang from the ground and cleared the back fence in one movement. Before the officers could even contemplate climbing over the top themselves Hopkins was two properties away, slipping between trees in the pitch dark. To him it was a well-worn track that didn't require illumination. Peattie and his crew were quite impressed. But the chase was on at the other end.

Three chase cars were waiting at Sydney Road, where Hopkins had first been sighted. Several minutes passed and there was still no exit from the point where he'd entered the row of backyards. The officers were becoming edgy. Suddenly Hopkins' red Laser roared down the hill behind them.

He'd emerged elsewhere and had reached his car without interception. He had about a 120-metre start and it was going to be difficult to keep pace once he got beyond Sydney Road. And so it proved; his car seemed to just disappear. The squad of detectives following the chase in Libby's lounge room yelled directions on the police radio, but no one knew where he'd gone. The camera crew had given chase as well, but he'd evaded the net. There was little point in going to his apartment, although he'd have to return home sometime. It was still possible Hopkins hadn't been aware that it was the police on his tail. Maybe he merely suspected the PI was back.

We packed up for the night, baffled, and took the last piece of equipment from the house. Libby closed the front door and went back inside. She said goodnight to her parents from the hallway and returned to her bedroom, totally exhausted. She slumped on the bed, on top of a television cable, too tired to care. Minutes later, her eyes sprung open to a flashing light out of the side window. Hopkins was back, in utter defiance.

'Go away!' she yelled. 'You sick bastard—go away!'

Her father came racing in to her room to see why she was yelling so soon after the men had left. He saw her huddled up against her bedhead, staring at the windows on the side wall. He couldn't see any light, or any other sign that Hopkins was there, but this time he fully believed her story, angered by her endless torment.

Over that weekend, the police sifted through a copy of our tapes. There was more than enough for a warrant, and a raid on Hopkins' work and home was planned for the middle of the week. The timing suited both camps. In the meantime a forensic crew worked on Libby's back fence, looking for fragments of clothing that may have matched Hopkins', to place him at the scene on the previous night. The fact that police had witnessed the appearance of his balaclava under the infra-red would strengthen the case, but the scientific team had to come up with fibres or footprints to nail their suspect. They would eventually obtain both, after matching physical evidence with that obtained in the forthcoming raid. As for Libby, she could tell that the police were moving mountains because of the pressure exerted by the television program. It was power she could only marvel at. While everything seemed to be moving at breakneck speed, she remained anxious about the airing of her story.

The feature report was to run in two parts, substantial coverage by prime time current affairs standards. It had been highly promoted over the weekend and the story contained more than enough salaciousness to promise compelling viewing. In the end, the show's senior producers elected not to identify Hopkins. There was still no forensic evidence to link Libby's stalker definitely to the man Phillip Hopkins. There was, however, plenty of time to make the link.

The images of his mask were so mysterious, so integral to the story, that it was felt that by not revealing his identity, the intrigue would entice viewers to come back for more. The first report was aired at 6:32pm, on 1 July 1996.

14

A LITANY OF COURAGE

Within ten minutes of the report airing, both *A Current Affair* and Manly Detectives received at least two dozen calls from women who thought they knew who the stalker was. They were mostly victims, some in tears, telling the phone operators that Libby's story resembled their own. These were harrowing stories of abuse, terror, persistent fright and, the common thread, frustration over the ineffectiveness of the countless AVOs they'd taken out. Most of them knew their man only too well. 'That's Phillip Hopkins, I know it is,' said one woman, who demanded to be put in contact with Libby.

'This is exactly what that nasty bastard did to me. That's Phillip for sure,' said another, happy to be interviewed for the follow-up report.

A wealth of information came in on Hopkins' nocturnal exploits and Peattie and Jane Hansen exchanged the names and details of the callers. Once the information had been examined, it transpired that at least four young women, all former girlfriends of Hopkins, could accurately identify their stalker. They'd all experienced the same violations and wanted to seek revenge. Between the show and Detective Sergeant Peattie, the girls were kept busy in the days that followed. They had to take time off work to make statements to the police or record on-camera interviews with Jane Hansen for Channel Nine. For all of them it was a rather hectic and nerve-racking couple of days, but one they all hoped would finally bring justice into their fractured lives.

Ashley Merton's story had some eerie similarities to Libby's. Phillip picked her at her friend's party—a fancy-dress affair, with bondage as the theme. During the party, Phillip stared at every woman who walked his way. Ashley remembered being attracted to his eyes, the same eyes she now hated. The night turned lustful, and she'd had too much to drink to drag herself back from the inevitable. The pair left at around 2:30am. He drove her back to his place. It was a night of sex, during which Ashley felt that Phillip was a bit too full-on, too dominant in bed. That included treating her roughly.

Interestingly, Phillip had a sidekick with him that night. His friend had taken a woman from the party home too, a woman who later told her girlfriends that Phillip's friend had a cruel appetite for full-on bondage sex.

Ashley had been seeing Phillip in the month immediately after Libby had been assaulted, when she'd first taken out the AVO. The police realised that if Ashley's recollection of events during her time with Hopkins was accurate, they could match up his movements to his nights off from stalking Libby.

Ashley told of a wild month and a relationship primarily based on sex, in which Phillip could never deal with rejection. He was short on talk, and focused on the physical. Even during a cup of tea, it was clear where his mind was heading. 'He wouldn't take "no" for an answer,' Ashley explained.

Ashley was never able to find out too much about Hopkins. He hardly mentioned his past. His background was largely a mystery to Ashley, although she'd established how wealthy his parents were and how pressured Phillip felt to succeed.

She then learnt through a discussion with a mutual friend, that Phillip was two-timing her, probably right from the start. His drunken conversations gave him away; he talked about a Louise Dent, an old girlfriend, and Ashley was immediately suspicious.

His persona too began emerging as fake. All too often, in response to Ashley sharing stories of old loves or outside interests, Phillip would simply agree with her observations, again and again, in order to highlight how compatible they were. But she could see through him, and she felt he didn't even really believe himself.

'He began turning up drunk and late, which is when I ended it,' she revealed. 'But he wouldn't accept the end, and became quite aggressive.'

Soon after, he began to stalk her, in spite of her repeated calls, telling him to get out of her life. He'd wait for her in the shadows outside her home after work. He'd turn up in car parks, emerging from between cars to taunt Ashley about 'losing out'. He'd enjoy scaring her when she least expected him to be there. Late at night, his face would appear from nowhere at the kitchen window and she'd drop the dishes she was washing in the sink, breaking them in fright. Even when the neighbours heard a noise and scared him away, he'd be back for more, for another chance to frighten Ashley again.

'He had me shaking like a leaf ... and when I screamed "What do you think you're doing?" he answered, "I've never done this before; it's the first time." A strange thing to say at any time. It was as if he supsected I knew he was an experienced stalker.'

The almost daily—and nightly—intrusions forced Ashley to move out of her unit to escape from him. But her ordeal also coincided with his arrest for stalking Libby Masters, cutting her treatment short.

Ashley couldn't explain why Hopkins was so compulsive and intense towards the end. Maybe it was his fear of being alone. After all, he had women lined up one after another, and in the gaps between. To her, he had an ego that could not handle rejection.

As the police questioned Ashley further though, bits of the puzzle, clues as to Hopkins' movements on notable nights, were falling into place. Asked about his predilection to arrive late, or not at all, Ashley told them of the series of nights when he'd arrive at her flat late, using the excuse that he'd been swimming at Willoughby Leisure Centre. This was early in their relationship, and Ashley was not comfortable about quizzing his story, but she knew something wasn't right. There was no smell of chlorine in his hair or on his body.

He was lying, and the dates she supplied matched perfectly with the nights he came to Libby's, only to take off without reason and without attempting to gain entry to her property. It made sense, he had other commitments but all the while, squeezed as much out of his nighttime schedule as possible to be with as many women as possible, even as their unwanted visitor.

'I'm terrified of him,' she told them.

Then there was Louise Dent, 24, a corporate finance executive, another victim from the lower North Shore, who'd met Hopkins at the funky inner-city club called CBD. The pair met after a friend of his hooked up at the bar with one of her friends. They had computers in common and got talking about the use of breakthrough software for various purposes.

She accepted a lift home and he came inside for coffee. It seemed Hopkins rarely used his own apartment to entertain his chosen women. Conversation on the lounge led to kissing and the dalliance ended lustfully, in her bed. The sex infuriated Phillip, because Louise failed to reach orgasm, a failure he took personally.

They did find common ground in their relationship, Louise thought, with both enjoying the other's professional determination and capacity. Louise felt that she had a similar personality to Phillip and she respected his proclaimed love of drama and singing.

Hopkins seduced Louise Dent at about the same time as Ashley. They both just happened to have friends and acquaintances that blew the lid on Hopkins' bed-hopping ways. Louise's tale was not one of stalking, just shonky stories, shocking lies.

'He lies a lot; it's his standard way of living,' she told police. 'I've just found out that he was also seeing Ashley, a third person let it slip the other day. He'd say he had to go away for the weekend. For instance he once claimed he was going down to Bendigo for a seminar, but he must have been with her. I couldn't find him where he said he'd be. I know he was with her. We never really officially broke up, but I'll never see him again.'

Frances Mallard was a little older, 28 years old, a teacher. She'd met Hopkins a year earlier. Of all the women who came forward from the television story, Frances was the most livid.

Although their relationship was not strong, nor continuous, she had slept with Hopkins on one of the nights he'd been recorded turning up at Libby's. She recognised the dark sloppy joe and pants—he'd worn them to Frances' house that very same night.

The links didn't end there. In a comparison of events and dates, it emerged that Frances was indeed the woman Hopkins had been going out with when he first met Libby at the Oaks. It was she he'd spoken to at the bar.

Frances described a man not to be trusted. She never felt comfortable around him. He was supremely jealous, and his third-degree interrogations drove her insane. And although she was not a prime stalking target, he did refuse to accept that their relationship was over and pestered Frances with phone calls, public abuse and unwanted late-night appearances on her doorstep—often engineered to terrify. What was even more deranged was his frequent delivery of flowers, several bunches of them, even during periods of abuse and stalking. Frances told Detective Peattie that he'd once made a significant comment: 'We met a private investigator together, and Phillip said "I'd be good at that".'

There were now Libby, Ashley, Louise and Frances, all linked to Phillip at about the same time. His schedule was crammed with appointments, and even Peattie was stunned at his deception.

But there was one final interviewee, a woman who in the end didn't have to be persuaded to go public. She came forward to join forces with Libby and slam Phillip Hopkins so he could never dish up his foul treatment of women again. Simone Crowe had watched Libby's courage on television at home the previous night, and tears of pride rolled down her face. She was infused with determination. It was time to lend a proper hand and go public with her story too—a story as terrifying as Libby's, albeit past history now. It had to be told, not necessarily to verify Libby's testimony in a court case, but Hopkins had to be outed forcefully to the public and those close to him, for the last time.

Simone was interviewed and featured prominently in the follow-up story that would air two weeks later, which included the naming of Phillip as the stalker. She detailed everything, from the time he entered her life in 1987, the initial abuse and violence, to the jealousy, stalking and her own flight into the country and ultimately overseas. Simone's words were carefully chosen and she didn't skip details. She recalled working in a pub, Hopkins tailing her in and out of work, throwing beers at her, abusing her, never leaving her alone. Simone explained how her flatmates over those years moved out in fear, and friends simply vanished because of the torment he heaped upon anyone close to her. He threatened to commit suicide. The picture of terror she described was compelling. Her demeanour on camera was focused but relaxed. This was an exorcism, victims gathering together for a common purpose. The power was all theirs this time; the thunder of the law was only a step or two behind them.

Late on the afternoon of Tuesday 2 July, Jane and her television crew were called to Hopkins' apartment. They'd been close to the location for several hours, waiting for the police. Earlier, in front of an office full of colleagues, police had raided his work premises, seizing his computer terminal and arresting him without regard for the embarrassment it was causing. His workmates were in a state of shock.

Back at Hopkins' apartment, police weren't leaving anything to chance. With the eyes of a national audience on the case, this was a warrant that had to be justified. Even the smallest piece of evidence had to be uncovered. To that end Peattie brought Hopkins back to his flat, and requested another member of his family be informed and attend before items were taken from the premises. Hopkins was initially against informing anyone until Peattie spoke to him about what lay ahead. 'This is not another fun AVO, son,' Peattie said quietly. 'We now have witness statements a mile high ... allegations beyond what Libby has against you, mate. Not to mention physical evidence which the scientific team here will clobber you with by the end of the week. There are no secrets anymore, son. The media is about to reveal who you are to millions of people. It's over mate, you're goin' to jail, so call your mum now before it's too late!'

When Kathryn Hopkins arrived, Phillip and his mother embraced, close to tears, in the lounge room of his unit. But Phillip remained bolshy towards the police, using less than convivial language as they took him into the various rooms of the house.

They found a black balaclava, several private investigator's handbooks, two torches, three surgical gloves and the newspaper article featuring a disguised photo of Libby. The forensic crew removed three pairs of running shoes from his wardrobe and several Sloppy Joes from the drawers and dirty clothes basket.

As the items were seized, bagged and marked in the main room, Hopkins became irate, shouting that the police had 'loaded him up and put the items in his room'. Peattie ignored his protests and spent almost an hour completing the search.

As officers escorted Hopkins from the apartment block, Jane was there to fire questions at him and film his arrest. Detective Peattie gripped Hopkins' handcuffed elbow. There'd be no hitch in this arrest, not in front of the cameras. The original story had created an enormous amount of interest, including much discussion on talkback radio. It wasn't Detective Sergeant Peattie's biggest brief, but it was shaping up to be the most closely watched, and, although he was not one for the media spotlight, he had no choice but to follow this through to the end. Apart from ensuring that the preparation of evidence and prosecution was seamless, he'd also begun to develop a rapport with Hopkins' victims and was determined to secure a conviction.

Back at Manly Police Station, Hopkins was taken to the central interviewing room at the detective's office. As soon as Peattie returned to the main part of the office, the supervising uniformed sergeant was waiting to see him. He gestured that the pair needed to talk privately, inside Peattie's own office. The officer in charge told Peattie that he was required to answer what is known as a ministerial memo that had been faxed to the station soon after the Hopkins family was informed of Phillip's arrest. The officer informed Peattie that the Police Minister wanted an immediate response. Either someone had made a complaint regarding the raids or the minister was anxious regarding the media attention the arrest was about to attract. Peattie saw red. He'd had to answer complaints before from well-heeled individuals whose family members had found themselves on the wrong end of the law, but never had he received a ministerial memo so soon after an arrest.

'Tell them I'll handle it later. I've got a crook to interview.'

'Not gonna happen, Ray. The fax was followed up by a call from the commissioner's office. They want a response now. They want you to answer the memo immediately mate—interview the crook afterwards.'

Peattie knew he was snookered and thought about the distraught and angry women he'd interviewed in the past few days. He couldn't let them down and wouldn't allow this brief to be taken out of his hands. It dawned on him how seriously some in Macquarie Street were treating the case. The media pressure no doubt added to their interest. He was more worried at this point about getting Hopkins into the interview room than saving his backside, before his family or legal team had time to talk him out of cooperating.

This is putting the bloody cart before the horse, he thought. He was angry but had no alternative. He cobbled together a rough response to the minister, defending the legitimacy of the arrest and search of Hopkins' flat. As he frantically signed the response, forensic police gave Peattie the last piece of the puzzle: confirmation that clothing fragments taken from Libby's fence visually matched those seized in the raid on his apartment. Hair strands taken from the same clothing would undoubtedly synch up with several caught on a rough part of the palings. That left his footprints; they were able to make a clear match between the soul prints on shoes at his apartment to those removed from the muddy prints inside her property, where he'd jumped onto the ground. Together with the damning evidence of phone-line tampering under Libby's floorboards, these last pieces of the puzzle completed a compelling scientific picture. A court could not ignore the facts—if assembled properly. The police had even kept that old piece of pizza, which roughly matched dental records obtained by court warrant.

Two national media stories had been aired, a long list of witnesses interviewed and the police brief against Hopkins was strong. His charges included a series of stalking counts under the new legislation, which carried a maximum five-year jail term or $5000 fine. He was also charged with contravening a domestic violence order—taken out by Libby—on three occasions, unlawful entry three times and being disguised by mask with intent to stalk.

In the short term Detective Sergeant Peattie had enough to put Hopkins away behind bars. It wasn't the local bail sergeant that would get in his way; it was the legal system and all its adversarial nuances he was worried about. How would his brief stand up against a rich kid's defence team? If justice meant anything, it must be prepared to stand up for Libby and the other victims, and send a message to Hopkins and those like him.

The ministerial memo prevented him from speaking to Hopkins early enough to get anything from him. In the company of his father and local defence attorney, Hopkins refused to answer any questions. Bail was refused and Hopkins found himself in a prison van on his way to Long Bay gaol, and his first night as a prisoner of the state of NSW. And Libby, for the first time in months, would have a peaceful night's sleep.

PART FOUR:
A LONG TIME COMING

15

IN THE VICE

'Not guilty you're worship,' bellowed one of Sydney's top silks, Maxim Pincott QC, at the magistrate, Alan Moore.

It was mid-July 1996 at the Manly local court. The well-to-do Malcolm Hopkins had hired a legal monolith to defend his son. There was no expense spared. His approach was full-throttle and he didn't plan to leave the court without his clean-cut, private school-educated son Phillip, discarding the title of 'the prisoner Hopkins' and regaining a clean slate. Or rather a cleaner slate … there was nothing he could do about Phillip's brushes with the law several years ago, nor his escape from lawful custody and bond for assault. Money couldn't wash those deeds away.

After the local prosecutor had gone through the charges and statement of facts, up rose Maxim Pincott QC like a Goliath ready to pulverise his David. The argument was forceful, albeit predictable: this was the fantasy of a mentally-ill young woman, who had never recovered from his client's rejections, and only sought to besmirch all that he had left, his reputation.

The QC vowed to prove two very important points; that Libby was still intent on drawing Phillip Hopkins back into her web, and that she was indeed suffering from a mental illness. Additionally, he maintained, the video evidence available to the court had been fabricated by television producers hell-bent on claiming a scalp and making headlines with a big-rating exposé. Libby was using the media to put his client behind bars.

'Pure prime time fantasy your worship. They are past masters at this,' snorted Pincott.

Detective Peattie could smell a rat. It was a curious boast to say she was dragging him back into her web: what did they have that could prove that? And how was he planning to determine her current state of mind? 'This'll be interesting,' Peattie whispered to his partner.

'This man has become the victim. He denies any knowledge of stalking,' Pincott continued. 'They have the wrong man.'

Libby, meanwhile, was outside the court, sitting silently, motionless, on the bench near the front steps. She'd probably be called on day one but was not entitled to hear any of the summary opening addresses or any evidence from police witnesses.

Pincott summed up his opening by alleging suspicious police collusion over the recorded material, a heavy-duty accusation to make in any court. Peattie was bristling, his offsider was half out of his seat, and the prosecutor was politely objecting before any evidence had even been presented.

'Those are fairly tall claims,' replied Magistrate Moore.

'Under the circumstances, Your Honour, both valid and justified.'

The fight was on. Pincott knew he needed to force the police and their star witness to scramble under attack and if required, a degree of intimidation would be necessary. This case was certainly not going to be handed to Pincott on a plate. But that was his stock in trade; the learned QC had made quite a career out of snatching victory from probable defeat. He needed to adopt a 'kill or be killed' approach, and the aggressive tactics had only just begun.

Libby was not called to the witness box until day two, after a problematic first day for the prosecution, during which Pincott tried to fry the detectives and forensic officers who took the stand. What was normally standard local court procedure, to verbally present their written statements, became a joust, a tormented argument with a superior debater. Pincott had made some of Peattie's underlings look shaky, scrambling to cover the holes in their evidence. It was not a good start and the attack dragged on for almost the entire day. They clearly hadn't expected the minute details to be examined so meticulously. But this was a wearing-down process, echoing Hopkins' own technique.

'Libby Masters to court one,' yelled the sheriff from the double doors to the courtroom.

Libby was jolted out of her trance. Her body was already shaking from the cold wind blowing off the harbour, but the call to the stand had her literally trembling.

From the outset, the police prosecutor made every attempt to make her feel comfortable, from allowing Libby to discuss her role at work to how long she'd spent with her family at their current abode and how often she visited the Manly Swim Centre. The calm and measured atmosphere he was creating was disturbed for her by two strange sights directly in front of her in the courtroom.

Sitting on the front defence table, immediately beside the distinguished QC, was a ruddy-faced woman, dressed in a pin-striped women's business suit. The most alarming aspect of her presence were the woman's piercing eyes, which appeared to be trained directly and incessantly on Libby. It was a look of disdain and revulsion, which had Libby's heart pumping. She felt she was being psyched out.

To top it off, there, just a few metres in front of her, to the QC's left, sat Phillip Hopkins. It had been so long since she had seen him last, seen him without a balaclava at least and in daylight.

It was not only Phillip's presence that unsettled Libby, however, it was the pathetic way he was attached to his mother that shocked her most. He was laying his head on Kathryn Hopkins' lap like a scolded dog looking for a pat. And he was getting that pat—his mother's hand was caressing his temple. Libby knew only too well how Kathryn treated her son, but this stunned her.

This is a freak show, she thought, her focus lost, before trying to pick herself up and get back to the job of giving her evidence clearly and convincingly.

After a little less than one hour, the prosecutor was done. An adjournment was suggested, but Pincott was having none of it. This was his chance to devour the young woman, who was tired and needed a break. He hardly laid eyes on Libby as he questioned how her ordeal had affected her. Was it causing nightmares, strange thoughts?

'All the time, yes. It's crazy,' she said, almost relieved that her enemy was at last recognising her plight and the pressure she'd been under. She had let her guard down so easily. 'Crazy' was exactly the word Pincott was looking for.

'Crazy? Like unstable?' asked Pincott. 'It must be enough to drive you crazy, what with the late nights, the supposed visits in a mask by your awful boyfriend. What a nightmare, you must have needed help.'

With that, Pincott approached the witness. 'You needed help, right?'

'Yes, I did,' she agreed reluctantly.

'Yes, go on. Help from whom?' pressed Pincott.

'I saw a psychiatrist,' she said quietly. 'I just had to see someone.'

'Speak up, young lady!' Pincott bellowed, jolting every person in the courtroom out of their seats.

'Yes, I did. I had to see someone.'

'You're seeing a psychiatrist right?' pressed Pincott again.

Before Libby could answer, Pincott produced a series of surveillance photos showing Libby entering and leaving the premises of a psychiatric doctor's office in Neutral Bay, on no less than four occasions. In several of those photos, Libby clearly appeared openly distressed as she left the premises, an emotional wreck. These were personal moments, made grossly public. Her privacy had been invaded yet again, and this time for many more to see. She'd been stalked by the very system that was meant to protect her.

'You've been following me?' she asked Pincott, interrupting his address to Magistrate Moore.

'Yes, young lady, we need the truth, and the truth seems to come in short quantities from you!'

An objection was lodged and sustained. Pincott apologised for his curt remark. But from this point on, Pincott used Libby's now officially fragile state to highlight how unreliable her testimony could be.

'Well, with all the mental trouble you were experiencing at the time, it's a wonder you could tell what was happening, who was knocking, who was responsible,' he said, as he grilled Libby on aspects of what she saw on the nights when Hopkins was allegedly recorded entering her property.

She could not verify most of the sightings *A Current Affair* had recorded because she wasn't monitoring the cameras when the intrusions occurred. Pincott tried to discredit Jane Hansen and me, as he fought his case based not on the evidence but on the credibility of those who supplied it. The questioning Libby faced was intimidating and gruelling, made even worse by the stares she continually received from the woman in the pinstriped suit in front of her. Phillip too remained a distraction, as his mother hand-combed his hair. It was a three-pronged assault that had Libby's head spinning. She was mentally spent, exhausted from the rapid-fire attack. She was powerless to fight, to win any of the points Pincott was raising.

Suddenly, Pincott turned to confer privately with Phillip's father, and then asked for an adjournment of 24 hours. This was extended due to the court's commitments in the week ahead. Libby's part in the process was now over. The police prosecutor thanked her, then Jane Hansen met her outside. I'd been called away on another assignment, but Jane had just returned from directing her crew as they followed Hopkins' parents out of court, to the car park at the rear.

Jane heaped praise on Libby and told her that her arguments had stood up well. Libby looked drained and said she was heading straight home to hibernate. Being briefed by the prosecutor, four hours in the witness box and three days in and out of court had taken its toll. She said she could not return to the court for a minute longer. 'I don't care any more. If that's what you've got to go through to get justice, why bother? Why would any woman bother? That almost killed me in there.' Tears welled up in her eyes.

Peattie also came over to express his support and thanked Libby for her brave effort in the witness box. She asked that someone call her when the result was eventually known. Libby declined the offer of a lift home. Not to be chased or harassed every second day was one of Libby's recently won freedoms—and she wanted to make the most of it, in spite of leaving court a tired, defeated mess.

When she reached the bottom of the steps, a hand touched her on the shoulder from behind. She was startled and turned quickly to see who it was. She had no idea who the woman was.

'I'm Simone, Libby. Simone Crowe.'

The women immediately embraced, tears in their eyes. Their hug lasted a long time. Theirs was a bond even they barely understood. It didn't matter that they had never set eyes on each other before. They were victims to the same tyranny, linked by a relentless quest for justice.

'You were amazing in there,' Simone whispered. 'I was right down the back. You didn't see me. He can't get out of this now. He's gone—and you did it. You did it for everyone. You're a bloody star!'

'Stop it. I just did what I could. I just kept going,' Libby replied.

'Just like him,' replied Simone.

They spoke about what was likely to happen to Hopkins. Simone said she felt a compulsion to be at the court, to see him take a fall. Libby thanked her for her help and told her that she had played an important role in keeping her 'up' and 'hopeful'. They parted as friends, connected by grief.

The court reconvened several days later, and it didn't take long before Pincott was taking an aggressive tack. The chips were down: the scientific evidence was solid; Libby was an authentic witness; the recorded tapes were clearly not doctored. In a dramatic and sudden turnaround, Pincott raised the white flag and Hopkins changed his plea to guilty. He'd lost the battle to be exonerated and had been humiliated beyond comprehension by a woman who just wouldn't stay down for the count.

'Guilty as charged then,' said Magistrate Moore.

'I find the offences proved and a conviction on the assault is now applied too, as the previous bond conditions dictate. I think we need to seek some psychiatric assistance for Mr Hopkins, Mr Pincott. I'd like to see a report in a week. I'll take submissions from both sides in a fortnight, and I'll have a sentence for your client on the nine charges after that. If you're applying for bail, don't bother; it's refused. Mr Hopkins, you can expect some time incarcerated. Case adjourned!'

A wide smile came over Detective Peattie's face. I leaned over immediately and slapped the officer on the back in an expression of joy.

We were all over the moon, not just because we'd helped beat the crook who'd made so many lives so miserable, but we'd been up against stiff opposition: the big-city QC under instructions to beat up on the key witness. Hopkins' temporary jail term would now be extended: the magistrate had made that clear. Libby had gone through so much. She'd found the most radically public way of forcing the police to act, and that took guts. We were all so pleased for her; our admiration for her tenacity was beyond words.

Late that day, I eventually made contact with Libby at home. She'd been out for most of the afternoon, unable to sit at home waiting for the phone to ring. She'd been through too much already. I told her the good news: 'He's put up his hands and pleaded guilty, Libby. He's going to jail for sure! You've done it ... you've got him. He can't get out of this now. He's gonna get what he deserves. This is such a gutsy win for you. Well done!'

At first Libby wasn't sure what she was hearing. But soon it sank in that the case was indeed over and that her story had been proved undeniably to be true. She could no longer be accused of lying. 'If only I could see his face,' she said. 'He can't hide his face now.'

Her relief was palpable. It was the vindication that so often during her ordeal she had thought she would never achieve. This was a hard-won victory.

At that very moment, Phillip Hopkins was once again in a Corrective Services van, herded up with four other prisoners, on his way to begin his long-term stint in the harsh confines of Malabar's Long Bay Gaol ...

Libby's mother and father had walked the ruined path that their daughter had taken. They'd experienced the helplessness of her plight, the sleepless nights. They had witnessed her frustration with the legal system and the very public stance she had taken. They did what Libby wanted throughout; they kept their distance and trusted her instincts to solve her own problems. But even they were flushed with relief. In a touching letter to reporter Jane Hansen, Libby's mother expressed how appreciative the family was of the work done by Jane and myself in 'very trying circumstances'. She wrote: 'Our family is greatly relieved and able to sleep soundly at night, which we have not done for quite some time. Thank you.'

I could see then the impact of stalking not only upon the lives of the victims but also for those who love them so very dearly. It was clear too that Libby's parents had never been more proud of their daughter.

16

A MAD MIND

Two weeks had passed since the verdict and Hopkins' grief at being inside indefinitely had begun to abate. He managed to keep out of trouble in Long Bay, and after a while was back doing what he felt comfortable with—seducing his women, this time by remote control.

His target this time was Louise Dent, the 24-year-old corporate finance executive who had never actually been stalked by Phillip and had not had the opportunity to build up the same animosity towards him as some of his other victims. They'd never really broken up and, in spite of his strange behaviour, she told police that they had established some kind of 'life connection'.

The fourteen-notebook-page-letter he wrote to her gave the clearest insight yet into the stalker's deranged mind:

Dear Louise,

Hello Louise. I've given a lot of thought to whether I should write to you or not and now that I've decided, I'm finding it hard to start. I guess I should start with a few admissions; and allow me to include some explanations as to why I thought it better to mislead you at the time—and then I would like to inform you of the truth and the absolute facts as to where I am, why I am here, and for how long I'll be here and how my life has changed for the better—perhaps not now; but what I have been through will change the way I will live my life in the future.

I'm in Long Bay Gaol. I have been since 2 July. I'm 30 years old, Louise—never been in trouble of this magnitude before. In fact, in any trouble at all with the law. This time twelve months ago, I would never have thought it possible—even one month ago.

Admission #1—I lied to you about where I was on 3 July on the phone. I wasn't in Victoria, and I know a little about PABX lines, which is why that lie came so easily. #2—I also lied to you the week before about me being sick and so not able to watch *Melrose Place* with you, or see you at all. Although I wasn't feeling too well!—I was at Manly Court hoping like hell I would get bail. This didn't eventuate and I was promptly loaded in a prison van and taken to jail. Incidentally, my Supreme Court bail application a week later also failed—no thanks to statements coming from left, right and centre from panic-stricken girls that had revealed some unfounded private and minor incidents in the occasionally [sic] very short time I knew them and/or from people I thought were my friends and has [sic] continued to be up until now. Or in particular from a girl I went out with for two years, ten years ago. I don't blame them so much actually—more the police method of questioning. And I don't blame you for yours. Although I would like you to forgive me for 'lying a lot' and perhaps consider seeing me again soon.

And that's about it! No more lies; no more admissions. Now it's time for some facts. The charges I've been faced with since meeting Libby Masters in August last year are: assault in December and stalking between January and June. On advice from my solicitor, Mr Trevor Nyman—who commands $3000 a day for his services (so far my father has paid in excess of $20,000 in barrister's fees since January), I have pleaded guilty on all charges. Why? Technically, by the law and Libby's and other's testimonies and statements, I did assault Libby. We had a horrific argument on my birthday which resulted in me tearing her dress and grabbing and dragging her up her street.

There is a lot of irony in this Louise. She used to punch, kick, slap and choke me constantly in our six-month relationship—which was the most hostile, dysfunctional and scary relationship I've ever had.

Very similar in nature to the two-year relationship I had with Simone Crowe, which ended in 1988. It's difficult to remember a lot about that. Perhaps another time. But I've had plenty of relationships between Simone and Libby without a complaint. I can't really explain why but I suppose there is a certain kind of personality that clashes with mine in a violent, aggravating way. I've had the unfortunate experience of being in a two-way addiction with such a 'personality' twice in my lifetime. Believe me; I'll be able to see the warning signs if such a person enters my environment again and pull out quickly—before it becomes all-consuming and hurtful to both sides.

I'll admit to you, Louise, that when both relationships finally ended I did behave somewhat irrationally. I've sent flowers, letters and appeared unexpectedly where I knew they would be. I found it hard to fall out of love (or addiction) as quickly as they did. Probably if they were honest they would say that they were just as bizarre in their behaviour during and after the break up—but that's another irony I have to live with.

But let me tell you some more facts. I have never threatened to kill either one, or their relatives—contrary to Simone's statement. I never threatened to commit suicide, also contrary to Simone's statement. I have never tampered with Libby's telephone line. The calls she made to me and their durations and content are all documented by Telstra for anyone to peruse. I have never donned a balaclava and jumped over Libby's fence into her backyard. Her statement claims that I have done so every night since January.

Before I go on—let me tell you a few things about Libby. About two months into our relationship—she found out during the course of one of our arguments that I had also been seeing Frances Mallard at the same time. She gave me a not-unreasonable ultimatum—to get rid of Frances. It just amazed me, Louise, just how history repeats. Ashley Merton gave me a similar ultimatum about you. I started to see a girl named Shelly and so started the decline of my and Simone's relationship eight years ago. How does this happen? After a lot of soul searching and personal examination of myself over the past three weeks, I can only answer that in a spiritual way. I believe God is telling me to clean up my act, to seek love and not lust, to trust and be trusted. These lessons I'll put into practice when I get out.

So what, you may ask? Libby may have seemed cool and together on *A Current Affair*, but I've had many friends who can vouch for wild changes in her persona. I give it to you also as an explanation for her vindictiveness towards me—combined with my unfaithfulness.

Louise, please don't think that I was habitually unfaithful in my 'previous life' before coming here. The fact is that Libby was also unfaithful. Twice we were both addicted to each other and both hoped that would turn into love—but also we were both looking for a way out—and being unfaithful was our way of doing that.

Simone was a similar story. I realise you may be looking for an explanation regarding you and Ashley—I can only say that Ashley seduced me at Frances' party and I fell for it. It was all happening so quickly, and believe it or not, my decision was to keep seeing you. Sure, it's true that Ashley had decided to dump me anyway after Friday, because I was expected at her place for dinner when I was with you. And it's true that I delivered flowers and probably scared her with my persistence but basically my pride was hurt and I was selfishly trying to repair that, as well as deal with the deja vu of it all.

God, I probably sound like a real male slut and ultimately chauvinistic—and I can see that now as well; but I have changed, Louise. Three weeks in the slammer will do that.

But there were other catalysts. As I said, the charge of stalking has been around since January. It was originally between two days. They see that I've been charged with assaulting Libby previously and as a result of my flower and letter sending and turning up on her doorstep—they slap on a stalking charge as well.

The hearing was part heard when all this started to happen—and looking very good for a 'not guilty' verdict. It was due for completion in August. The charge has since been amended by the prosecution to incorporate a six-month period from January to June. I'll talk about their evidence later.

A roving reporter who probably scans the local court proceedings regularly for *The Sun Herald* wrote a full-page article for that paper in early June. It outlined the 'horrors of stalking' in general—and used a lot of the details that were relevant to my case. This was the first examination of Libby's claims that somebody else made those 21 telephone calls, from her place to mine, via a tampered with telephone line. This story was concocted by her electrician, although Libby cleverly avoided this fact on *A Current Affair*.

This newspaper article used false names, but it was obvious that they had interviewed Libby—because there was evidence that was not allowed in court. (The telephone tampering theory was one—there were no fingerprints on the device!) Enter *A Current Affair* and one private investigator.

This private investigator first came to my attention when he repossessed my car in May. I think I told you of that incident. He was hired by Esanda—the company that I had my car loan through—to repossess my car because I had fallen behind by about a month, over an eighteen-month period. As per the contract I signed they were entitled to repossess. He did so under a barrage of insults and abuse from me at the time. This intrepid investigator, we assume, then looked at my criminal record, and saw that I was in the middle of a stalking hearing and an assault charge conviction against the one girl. Good stuff. He then offers his services to Libby.

We've seen his report—and for about a month this guy follows me around—and sees no evidence of me stalking anyone. He sees me going about my normal working and social life. Enter *A Current Affair* and the moralistic reporters that go with it. No payment has been forwarded to the investigator yet—because he hasn't seen anything worth reporting.

A Current Affair takes over the services of the investigator—they all put their heads together—and all of a sudden things start to happen in Libby's backyard. I will go so far as to say, Louise, that the entire video footage was acted out. There are other possibilities, but I'm sure that's what has happened. Libby called me that week at work and spoke six words and a lot of blubbering. 'I can't leave this alone now.' Click.

The video is then submitted to the police. The police need stronger evidence, the investigator knows this and so plants a balaclava, torches and gloves in my bedroom chest of drawers at home—on the morning of 2 July when he knows I'm at work and he knows the police will search my home later that day. He gets his fees, *A Current Affair* gets their ratings, and the police get a conviction with watertight evidence.

On top of this are numerous complaints from Libby that I had stalked her throughout the year, but which weren't acted on by the police.

Three events actually: the first occurred at the Oaks Hotel in Neutral Bay in February; the second occurred at the Metropole; and the third occurred at the Basement—I believe from memory in March and April consecutively.

The Oaks and Metropole incidents basically consisted of me coincidently running into Libby and attempting to rationalise with her. Keep in mind that both venues were places that she knew I frequented regularly—they were just up the road from where I lived, whereas she lived at Manly—a good 20 minutes' drive away.

The Basement incident was a similar scenario but with one notable difference. She called me the night before and enquired where I would be. I replied the Basement, and she duly turned up there! That night ended disastrously with another argument and the police being notified again by one of the bouncers.

I guess you're getting the picture of the prosecutor's case. Their investigations revealed nothing. They followed me one night in my car—*A Current Affair* filmed me driving from my parents' home to my home—but none of them saw me anywhere near Libby or her home. (Otherwise why not arrest me there and then?) The only one who says he saw me was the private investigator—who I've already stated is moral enough to plant a balaclava, torches and gloves in my home.

I've managed to explain it to you here (I hope!) in a few pages, but my case would take more than a week in a District Court to be heard. The police would call all witnesses who have given statements (including you!), and I would probably leave a 'reasonable doubt' in the magistrate's mind after the testimonies—and theories that I had stalked Libby. But I have no proof—and my alibis for where I was at the time wouldn't stand up. The prosecution, however, have one stark piece of evidence—the balaclava. If a magistrate found me guilty after a plea of 'not guilty', the penalty would be more severe than if my plea originated as guilty. And so my plea—guilty as charged!

And so *A Current Affair* reveals true identities and a dramatic 'confession'. Also the cost, Louise; we would be looking at a legal bill of $3000 a day for more than a week! For possibly no result!

So what now: the hearing is set for 15 August. My plea is guilty. The judge has three options. The best one is to release me straight away saying that six weeks that I've spent in jail is enough—go on your way! Or he may impose an additional sentence—community service or weekend detention or if worse comes to worse—more time in jail. (God help me!) That's the gamble we're taking.

What are we doing to help my cause? Well, I'm going through a probation procedure here over the next three weeks. I'll be examined by psychiatrists and psychologists and probationary people, to determine whether I'm over Libby, and whether I'm suitable for other types of sentencing apart from full-time jail. I'm sure their reports will be positive ones!

Also, I'm gathering together all my friends and family—and, believe me, they are all being extremely supportive—to produce affidavits, references, etc. All of this, and many of them in person, will be present before the magistrate on 15 August. I'll be there, in handcuffs, hoping to God I'm let go. Finally then I can put it all behind me. I'll be moving into my parent's home, changing jobs and taking along any friends who care to come along. I'd like you to be one of those friends, Louise.

I don't know when you will get this letter, Louise; the mail system here is really unpredictable. I have many more things I could tell you about life in here. Could you come and visit me? Be prepared for tight security and me being in a 'smuggle-proof' overall outfit, but I would love to see you.

So far every day I've been blessed with visits from family and friends. (Jason came today.) If you decide you would like to, please call the jail and speak to welfare. I'm only allowed one visit per day, and only one on weekends. You can also pass on any messages to me through welfare. I'm not sure of the number actually, but my details are: Phillip William Hopkins, 13 Wing.

Otherwise I'll assume you don't want to resume anything—or that you haven't received the letter. I have a feeling they do read and censor outgoing mail here. So I hope you'll forgive me if I call you when I get out and find out how you feel.

Hope you are keeping well, Louise.
Phillip xx

Louise didn't reply. Soon afterwards she received a phone call from Phillip, still in prison. She made it clear that she didn't want anything more to do with him. Nothing really scared her about Hopkins. She hadn't been trapped in his sticky predatory web, but she knew his uncanny powers of persuasion were dangerous and were capable of drawing her in, like the others she'd heard about. She couldn't trust herself and, considering what Hopkins was capable of, she did not make contact with him again.

17

RAISING THE GAVEL

The pre-sentence report prepared by a probation officer at Dee Why was a mixed blessing for Hopkins. The officer wrote that after six weeks inside, Hopkins' 'imprisonment has had a significant effect upon the offender'. As Hopkins negotiated the fierce culture of jail life, he 'expressed feelings of terror and intimidation'. He was recorded as saying, 'It is the worst experience of my life.'

Records showed that Hopkins was getting on 'reasonably well with prison officers and keeps away from any of the daily violence that ensued inside'. He spent several sessions with his probation officer, recording his inner feelings about Libby, relationships and his own inadequacies. 'I have some difficulties with relationships,' he admitted. 'I become addicted to women very quickly after forming an association.'

Hopkins would still not concede, however, that his behaviour in the first half of 1996 was his fault. He was 'victimised' and 'only pleaded guilty on legal advice'. Later, as the harsh reality of jail and the sobering realisation of his plight had begun to sink in, he retracted his statements of innocence. He accepted full responsibility for all his 'stupid and impulsive actions'.

On further examination he admitted to finding it 'difficult to accept guilt'. His probation officer concluded his assessment by stating: 'He is superficially well-mannered, with a problematic behaviour pattern.'

For reasons known only to Hopkins, he rekindled his Catholic faith inside prison and this change in direction was part of a report compiled by the prison chaplain. Hopkins had become close to a nun who'd made regular visits to selected prisoners and she reported that he had 'verbalised his regrets for his actions' repeatedly. Both members of the clergy were convinced that Phillip had a 'strong faith in God and wanted to make a fresh start', findings that Phillip's lawyers made sure were signed and highlighted in the hearings ahead.

The forensic psychiatrist who dealt with his case tackled the question of why he used a balaclava to frighten his victims in the middle of the night. This was integral to understanding Hopkins' treatment and disrespect for women. 'I asked him why, and he said he wanted to approach Libby to convince her to drop the charges,' the psychiatrist reported. 'He said he had his face disguised because he did not wish to be recognised by anybody else.'

Hopkins went further: 'I can tell you the motivation behind it all. Contrary to the assumption everybody is making, I have no intention of causing anyone any harm. I was attention-seeking and I wanted the attention of Libby. She was probably frightened; women are generally frightened because men are stronger and more aggressive. Women like this are very vulnerable.'

The psychiatrist concluded that Hopkins indeed had an obsession with Libby Masters. He clearly had a history of confronting relationship breakdowns with 'emotions equivalent to despair and devastation'. It was also written that he, 'handled rejection with anger, but was always able to differentiate between right and wrong'.

Hopkins expressed his inner feelings with a great deal of emotion throughout the process of assessment. It may have had some bearing on the final recommendation, 'that he should be released'. He could then access psychiatric treatment and it was somehow concluded that he 'would not pose a risk' to Libby.

The relationship, he told his handlers, was now over and he no longer felt animosity towards her. The psychiatrist's report was presented to Magistrate Moore, providing him with compelling reasons to view Hopkins in a new light.

Sentencing day arrived—15 August 1996. Libby was not present at Manly Court. She was wrung out from all the pressure and tension. The recent publicity had encouraged acquaintances to dredge up the drama over and over again when they met. They presumed their empathy was what she needed, but Libby just wanted to try and move on. She'd had enough. Despite all the positive predictions from the people around her, including we media, she somehow had a gut feeling that she'd be let down again. She felt she needed to brace herself against the realities of the NSW legal system. She didn't want to care; but she did, far too much. The pending decision would determine the life she would now lead.

Peattie too had endured an entire career being let down by sympathetic judges. He knew that a year behind bars was the best they could hope for.

The hearing began with the presentation of various reports submitted to the bench which were then read out, including a sworn affidavit from Malcolm Hopkins with a very explosive attachment. This was to be his attempt to highlight Libby's alleged spell on his son and explain his stress and chronic anxiety. It was an eleventh hour attempt to swing Alan Moore back in favour of Phillip Hopkins.

Peattie had known something like this would be coming. 'Here it is,' he whispered.

After a small debate about its admissibility, which the local prosecutor lost, the letter was submitted to the court. It was a letter, allegedly from Libby, apologising to Phillip for 'past mistakes', and reiterating her vow of 'everlasting love'!

The letter, allegedly written in October the previous year, was a scrawled three-page note. In part, it read:

Dear Philly,
You forgot your Chokito so I decided to send it over. I don't know why we argue, but I feel it has to do with the following things: constant tiredness, lack of exercise and seeing too much of each other. This is a hard one because, like you, I am kind of addicted to you too! ... I have slowed down on seeing my friends

because I want to have your trust in me that I love you and haven't got time for any male but you.

You feel resentment for my past mistakes. Yes, I made some mistakes and lied to you! You know I am sorry for this and wish I could change that. We will never trust each other if you constantly bring up these stupid things I have done and punish me over and over. If you can't get over that, stop the destructive pattern and stop seeing me. I really hope you can, Phillip, because I would miss you terribly.

I can be a moody bitch at times and I am trying to stop this. (PMS is hard!!) I am aware when I am being unreasonable, but find it hard to say I'm sorry sometimes.

I can honestly say that I adore you, think you are sexy and intelligent and miss you constantly when I am not with you.

I am going to put 100% towards you, because I think if we can get through it, we can be very happy together. We both want the same things out of life—love, fun, not too much work, children and really good sex!

I hope you will decide to put 100% towards us, Phillip—please don't force yourself.

I love you ...
Libby
xxxxxxxxxoo

P.S. Don't worry so much, you have a girl who adores you, thinks of you constantly and would die if you left her!!

The police prosecutor was having none of this. He presumed it was a fake and wasn't about to let the defence team get away with it.

'How about we get a handwriting expert in now and we'll see who wrote the letter, Your Honour? Libby Masters was not known to be a letter-writer and made no reference to writing such letters. She's not here to defend herself either, so how about we have the letter examined and if it's legitimate we have nothing to argue. If not, the prosecution will submit to the court that the defendant face further charges. If, in the circumstances of a mere sentence submission, such a thorough test is impractical, how then can this so-called letter be accepted as evidence?'

The previously in-control Pincott was flawed. He didn't expect opposition to a mere letter, let alone a killer punch from the normally calm police prosecutor. Pincott grabbed for some other papers in front of him, gabbled that Libby had been under stress and agreed very quietly that there was no need to have his client's letter subject to another few weeks of scrutiny. It was removed from his list of pre-sentence submissions. The big-talking, highly regarded QC was knocked for six and Peattie knew his prosecutor had scored a direct hit.

Phillip's father immediately turned to his son and whispered a short message. Hopkins pulled his head out of his mother's lap and sat very still. Peattie watched his reaction and presumed that the accused had just been quietly admonished. His mother looked concerned and his father was clearly unsettled. It was apparent that their faith in their son was slowly being eroded. They were unaccustomed to such ignominy.

The senior prosecutor had his turn and told of a crazed man, unable to leave Libby alone and capable of violence in relationships. He then used the testimony of all the other women who'd had the courage to come forward to police following the television story as a battering ram against any further attempt to mitigate Hopkins' guilt. The impact of so many stories so similar in nature was the final straw for Hopkins.

'Garbage!' Phillip muttered, audible to all in the court. This was his past emerging and it hit a raw nerve. It was a past he thought he'd buried, certainly one he thought would never be connected to Libby Masters. His violent deeds against Simone Crowe were a distant memory, nothing to do with what he was now facing. At least he had thought it was a memory. Now Libby had unearthed the past and thrown it back in his face—without even being in the courtroom—in front of his parents and friends. Magistrate Moore had to intervene to put a stop to Hopkins' utterances.

The court was reminded that Hopkins' assault on Libby had been proved. It would attract a conviction under the terms of his bond if the magistrate found any of the charges in the current case proven. He found

Libby's statement to be truthful and was supported by the AVO Simone Crowe had taken out against Hopkins many years earlier.

Magistrate Alan Moore slammed Hopkins for his relentless pursuit of power over Libby. Yes he needed 'help' he stated, but it was no excuse for the games he played. His violent tendencies made his nocturnal behaviour even more threatening and a custodial sentence was the 'only appropriate punishment'.

Hopkins was sentenced to a fixed term of imprisonment of six months. A gasp of shock echoed through the small courtroom from those on Hopkins' side of the gallery. Even backdated to his first night in jail, he would not be emerging until the New Year. It was one of the toughest jail terms ever handed down under the new stalking laws introduced to NSW three years earlier. It was nowhere near the maximum of five years, but it was still a significant sentence and almost satisfied the expectations of Detective Peattie. Hopkins dropped his head in resignation and disbelief. His parents were shattered.

'The sentence will include constant psychiatric counselling, both during his prison term and after his release. Take the prisoner away,' ordered the magistrate.

The sheriff of the court grabbed Hopkins' arm abruptly. Kathryn Hopkins sobbed in the arms of her husband. Their son was being forced to endure another four and a half months inside; they could barely control their grief. But there was no getting away from the truth; it was Phillip Hopkins who'd taken his own route to self-destruction; he only had himself to blame. Perhaps it was lucky one of his victims hadn't chosen a more violent course to end his constant stalking. Libby had certainly contemplated it many times.

Later that afternoon, a prison van took Hopkins west, along Epping Road, down onto Pennant Hills road and into O'Connell Street … to an even more spartan prison than he'd become used to: the old Parramatta Gaol. These cold, stony lodgings were to be Hopkins' crude home until his release.

'Congratulations, Libby,' I informed her by phone. 'He's gone until next year—six months inside.'

She drew in a deep breath, completely vindicated. It had been worth the public exposure and dogged fight in court after all. He'd earned a massive rebuke and Libby recognised how harsh his environment was about to become. This was a mighty victory for Libby Masters over a series of seemingly insurmountable obstacles. She had little to say to me except what sounded like a heartfelt thanks.

I handed the phone to Jane Hansen, who was quick to offer Libby support and they agreed to keep in touch. Their bond was strong. Jane had done everything in her power to publicly humiliate Hopkins and pressure the system to act appropriately. The women were bolshy comrades who'd taken on the aggressor and won.

In reality, although we all wanted to stay close, it was never likely to happen. It would keep her nightmare far too alive and real to be continually reminded of it by our presence. We arranged a get-together, which I repeatedly postponed because of work commitments. But knowing what it was we had in common, I just couldn't see any advantage for Libby anyway. We lost contact for near on a full decade.

As to the question of whether it was truly over, Libby knew that such a drastic punishment, in such a dangerous and fearful environment, would shake Hopkins like he'd never been shaken before. She knew he would be on the verge of breakdown: he would be forced to view his perpetual game for what it was: cruelty beyond comprehension, which no one should be forced to bear, let alone several women at one time.

Would he come back to take revenge? she wondered. It was possible. Right from the start of *A Current Affair's* involvement with her, I'd explained what a rock-solid insurance policy Libby was taking out by going so public. 'The world would always know who was threatening and frightening you,' I'd told her.

Libby had thought about that a lot since she was first approached by the program. She wasn't frightened of what might happen come his release on 2 January. Not yet anyway.

She knew Hopkins was now fully aware of the steps she was prepared to take to reclaim her life. Her support team was too influential for even his guile and skill. He was surely not prepared to risk being caught again, to face the ignominy of his guilt and, moreover, another round of incarceration.

As Libby cleaned up after dinner that night, her phone rang, just after nine. She wondered who could be calling now. She'd already spent much of the evening fielding calls of support, which had become a tiresome replay of the whole ordeal.

'Hello, Libby speaking.'

'Um, Libby is it?' It was a man's voice.

'Yes,' she replied cautiously. 'Who's this?'

'It's Sergeant Kennedy here, from Mosman Police.'

It was the officer who'd given Libby a stern talking to about not wasting police time when Hopkins' defence produced the Telstra records appearing to show that she'd been harassing him.

'Yes, go ahead,' she said.

'I just wanted to call to say you are a brave and inspiring young woman, Libby. That's all. I was wrong to think you staged this case and I apologise unreservedly. All of us at the station apologise. We were wrong, and we all want you to know how sorry we are. You have got this bastard, no thanks to us … That's all.'

Libby was speechless. Her lip quivered; she found herself weak with emotion. It was an unnecessary, but touching gesture, which brought a tear to her eye. The call capped off a long and harrowing twelve months, and the words she'd just heard were more genuine than any she'd heard that day.

The embarrassing calls to police, their continual eye-rolling upon being called out at night, had stayed with her like a thorn all this time. The call she'd received was as cleansing as any prison sentence or television story. It gave her back her dignity; she was known to be a woman who told the truth. It was the perfect end to the most imperfect part of her entire life.

Malcolm Hopkins had taken his son's sentence hard. Whatever it took, he was going back to court to appeal. The cost was not a consideration. His wife's heart had been broken, and any consolation they could get during this dark time in their lives would be worth whatever they paid for it.

The appeal went to the Downing Centre within three weeks of Hopkins' sentencing. It was a quick turnaround that had even surprised police. They suspected that Malcolm Hopkins had used his influence to expedite the matter, but it was pure supposition. A new silk had been briefed for the appeal: Clive Steirn QC. The case was brought before District Court Judge Joseph Phelan. The Hopkins family could not have hoped for a better roster. Detective Peattie told his colleagues that he felt the QC Steirn must have gone judge shopping to extract something from a messy, lost case.

After just over four hours, during which no witnesses were called, only briefs submitted, Judge Phelan had developed firm views on the case. He was unconvinced about the phone tampering, despite the evidence, and was dissatisfied with the lower court's ruling. His words from the bench began in an encouraging way for the police and prosecution.

'I think I am obliged to increase the earlier sentence,' he said. 'This is almost unappealable and I'm glad the charges were treated seriously from the start. Mr Hopkins breached orders and bail. This is unacceptable. I see evidence of letters and phone calls and attempts to contact those who should be protected under these orders. He may be sending himself to jail for a year. I need to increase the magistrate's penalty and I quash that decision of "six months fixed".'

The prosecutor turned slightly towards Peattie, as if to celebrate. The comments seemed contrary to Phelan's reputation, but he was happy to accept any addition. How heartening for the victims to know that the judiciary was so prepared to punish their tormentors.

'I sentence Mr Hopkins to twelve months' imprisonment ... ' Phelan said, before pausing. 'But I make this ruling by handing down a minimum sentence of three months' hard labour, backdated to the time of his first imprisonment. Furthermore, I order the Department of Corrective

Services to ensure that Mr Hopkins has psychiatric guidance inside and when he gets out. From that point, the prisoner will not assault, threaten, molest or stalk within 500 metres of Libby Masters.'

The gavel hit the bench, compounding Detective Peattie's absolute shock. He'd done a total about-face and, as they all knew, under Truth in Sentencing legislation, any prisoner serving a maximum of three years or less is automatically released on parole when the minimum expires. His appeal had reduced his sentence—his release date was only one month away! The police were not surprised by Judge Joseph Phelan's sentence. They knew their man. They had witnessed many defendants receiving rulings unpopular with the police. He'd given Hopkins an early exit card and it was a major blow to the prosecution, undoing the good work the lower court had put in place.

Peattie telephoned Libby later that afternoon and told her the outcome of Hopkins' appeal. Funnily enough, she was not overly concerned. It was three months off his sentence, but she remained focused on the three months of hell that Hopkins was currently enduring. She knew that she'd given him the fright of his life. His release would come all too soon, but surely he'd learnt some lessons from the brutality of prison life.

Part of her resignation may have stemmed from the fact that she had become almost desensitised to the court process. She was now adept at bracing herself for a less than favourable outcome. The conclusion of the District Court Appeal now signalled the official end to a very messy public case in which Libby had always been a very reluctant participant.

18

REMEMBER ME

On the day of Hopkins' release from Parramatta Gaol, he was more than ready to leave. He could barely contain himself when he entered the guard room to collect his few belongings. He quickly signed the appropriate paperwork and was escorted to the two sets of large, bolted cast-iron doors at the front of the ageing prison complex.

He'd been counting down the days ever since he first entered and was thirsting to experience freedom again. There was no doubt that he was desperate for it.

Libby was not too distracted by the significance of the day, but edgy enough to feel a little fragile as she ploughed through her work. The phone on her desk rang about mid-morning. There hadn't been many calls that day and, as it rang, she sensed it might be related to the release of Phillip Hopkins.

She stared at the phone for a short time, wondering whether a prison or police officer was calling to notify her of his release. She wasn't aware of any requirement for that to happen and quickly dismissed her musings as nervous paranoia and picked up the handset and answering as she would for any other, work-related call.

'Hello, Libby Masters speaking,' she said brightly.

There was a pause at the other end and, in the background she could here the sound of traffic and a hum of voices in the distance. Then there was a deep breath before that familiar voice came down the line:

'I'm out now. I just wanted to let you know that.'

There was no mistaking it; it was him.

'It's you! You can't call me, you know that. What are you doing?'

'I rang to tell you I won't be bothering you anymore,' replied the former prisoner Phillip Hopkins, in a plain, cold voice.

'Why are you calling me then?' she asked.

He didn't answer her question.

After a pause, the phone went dead.

EPILOGUE

For the players in this story, the decade after these events proved an eventful period. In 2001 the man who had finally put Phillip Hopkins away, Detective Sergeant Ray Peattie, was himself sent to jail for four years on charges of corruption. He was caught on tape taking bribes and overseeing some of his troops doing the same. He confessed to almost an entire career 'on the take', falsely prosecuting suspects and protecting major players in the heroin trade throughout Sydney, especially during his time as a Drug Squad detective. Another two officers under his command and attached to the Manly Detectives' Unit were caught red-handed, on tape, by the Police Integrity Commission and jailed for corruption too. Peattie has since been released.

In 2004 Phillip Hopkins' father Malcolm left his executive position on the board of a multinational insurance giant after a dramatic purge of directors and senior managers in the organisation. The company had been misfiring, losing potential profits and dropped the ball on a deal involving a major bank. The newly appointed CEO and Malcolm Hopkins didn't see eye to eye. He left with a golden handshake, retired and is not pursuing any directorships.

He did, however, provide financial backing to Phillip, in a small business he started soon after his release from prison. The venture met with mixed success.

Meanwhile, Libby Masters is living with her partner and their baby daughter in a Northern Beaches suburb. She says she had recovered from the memories of that period of her life ten years ago and is very happy, particularly in her new relationship. But as this story neared publication Libby Masters found it difficult to liaise on the project. She had good reason to. The memories, the heartache and the cruelty she suffered were not something she wished to share with her new family. Libby had moved on, but encouraged me to write her story. She has not experienced a single stalking incident since the day Hopkins was released from prison.

EPILOGUE

My only additional contact with the serial stalker came indirectly, through a phone call two years after his imprisonment to my desk at Channel Nine. A friend was enquiring about a Phillip Hopkins who she had a hunch had been the subject of one of my televised investigations. Her friend had 'connected' with Hopkins and she was concerned over a few inexplicable incidents early in their relationship. I was gobsmacked that his name would crop up again like this. Without hesitation, I warned her to instruct her girlfriend to dump Hopkins immediately before it went too far.

Hopkins has since married and is living with his wife and two children—a boy and a girl—in a middle class suburb in the northwest of Sydney. Police say there have been no reports of stalking using a balaclava in his area in the past ten years, nor has Hopkins been named as a suspect in any additional cases of stalking. He did find himself in court again in 2006, on a minor traffic infringement. It could be that Phillip Hopkins' involvement with Libby Masters proved to be a hard lesson, well learned.

The stalker's victims have been given fictional names.
They've been through quite enough.

The stalker's name is also fictional, to protect the identity of his long-suffering victims.

ABOUT THE AUTHOR

Chris Smith was born at Parramatta, NSW, in 1962. He has worked as a newspaper, radio and television journalist, covering stories in Australia, the United States and throughout Asia.

He is currently the host of Sydney's number one talkback show, on radio station 2GB 873, following a successful stint as the station's Program Director.

Prior to this Chris spent over a decade working in News and Current Affairs at both the Seven and Nine Networks, including a period as national Chief of Staff for *A Current Affair*. He also became the first foreigner to broadcast live to China, during a two-year stint with China Radio International in Beijing.

He's been the recipient of awards for journalistic excellence in both radio and television.

The inspiration for this book emanated from a series of stories he produced on stalking for the Nine Network. His first book was a biography titled *Beyond Heartbreak: The True Story of Lorraine Cibilic*, published in 1995 by Kangaroo Press.

www.ingramcontent.com/pod-product-compliance
Lightning Source LLC
Chambersburg PA
CBHW070537090426
42735CB00013B/3009